"If you are interested in the history of Sausalito, the floating homes community, and the iconic structures in the area this is the book for you. The photos and maps are great and help immensely identifying landmarks and points of interest."-*Katherine Entwisle*

"...a very lovely book that is well organized, full of interesting information, and wonderful stories. For anyone wanting to put their finger on the pulse of life of the Sausalito waterfront and surrounding area, both past and present, I highly recommend this book." –*Michael Morgan*

"After moving to Sausalito more than a year ago...I found myself wanting to know more about the area. Mitch Powers book was the perfect answer to my quest in an entertaining and well written little book. Fascinating details unfold with a precise narrative, taken from the rich history of Sausalito, including the extensive colorful modern floating homes community. Although it is perfect for anyone with plans to visit the area...I found as a new resident it brought to life an area I now call home." –*Mary Coral-Amasifuen*

"I thoroughly enjoyed this well written book. It is the perfect companion to those lucky enough to travel the waters of Richardson's Bay, and an informative and amusing guide to Sausalito, California for those visiting by land."–*Mark Gates*

Sausalito History & Guide

*Tours, maps plus histories of
Tiburon, Belvedere & Angel Island*

by Mitch Powers

Mariposa Publishing

Greenbrae, CA
Printed in USA
3rd Edition
Copyright 2017 by Mitch Powers

Written by Mitch Powers
Photography by Mitch Powers (otherwise as noted)
Floating Homes map courtesy Waldo Point Harbor
Cover design and layout by Mitch Powers
Email: Positiveoutlook1@hotmail.com

Books by Mitch Powers

The Giants' Last Tear

Big Mountain

Stealing Hearts

Pandapple

The Adventures of Tory Cat

Art In The Wild

Stand Up Paddle Instruction Book

*First Strokes: Kayak Touring for Sit-on Top
& Sit Inside Kayaks*

On The Road to Shambala

Contents

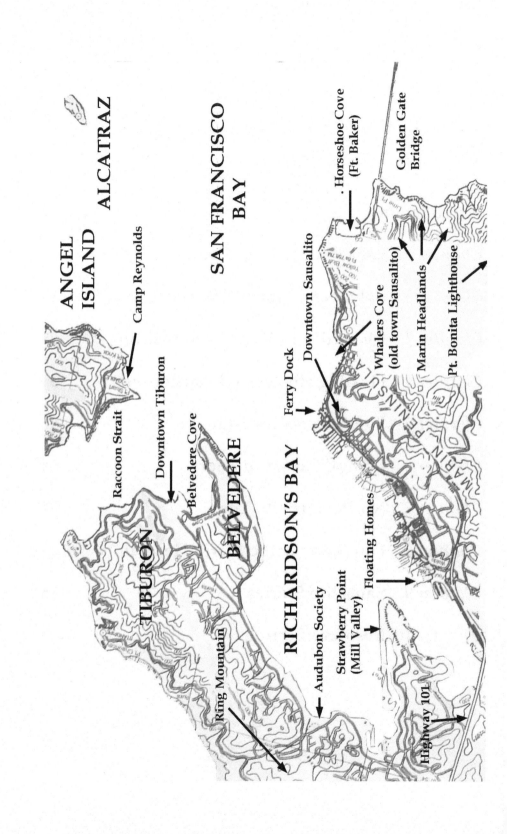

Introduction

This guide book is intended to enrich the experience of visitors and locals who'd like to learn more about the intriguing history of Sausalito, its vibrant waterfront and the surrounding communities. This dynamic waterfront is embraced by Richardson's Bay which also touches the shores of Strawberry Point (Mill Valley), Tiburon, Belvedere and opens up at its mouth to Angel Island and the greater San Francisco Bay. By reading this book you will get to know all these places.

With three tours (South, Central and North Sausalito) that take you along the waterfront, you'll become familiar with the rich, colorful history of Sausalito. To help you locate the sites discussed in each tour you'll find a map at the beginning of each section, and over 100 photos throughout the book. Also in the front of the book there is a general map to get your bearings, so take a moment to look at it. Exploring Sausalito can be done by walking, biking or driving. In addition, for those who seek an added element of adventure many of the historic sites, boats, the floating homes community, and wildlife can be viewed from the water. A kayak, Stand Up paddleboard or small skiff are great ways to go.

Although it's not necessary, I recommend you read the first several chapters before touring Sausalito. Since they offer a concise history of the town and nearby Tiburon, Belvedere and Angel Island, it will only enhance your understanding and enjoyment as you take off sightseeing. In addition, there is a chapter on Richardson's Bay natural history for the nature lovers in the group, and another on Sausalito's famous floating homes community and the always controversial anchor-outs. Finally, when you start the tours you'll get short descriptions of historic buildings, old ferries, classic boats, floating homes, WWII Marinship, Ft. Baker and the Marin Headlands while learning local stories.

Each tour has a starting point but with a careful reading of the relative map you can actually start exploring anywhere along Sausalito's main drag (Bridgeway), and start seeing specific sites highlighted in the book. I've included lots of physical addresses so if your GPS is on you'll be in great shape to locate everything.

In this third edition, besides all the new historical references and points of interest, I've extended the tour range to include Fort Baker and the incredibly beautiful Marin Headlands. Both are full of history with dramatic panoramic views of the Golden Gate Bridge and coast line. Pound for pound the drive (or bike for the hearty) up Conzelman Road in the Marin Headlands offers some of the most stunning scenery on the California Coast.

The last two chapters cover Sausalito Stories such as the origins of Otis Redding's *Sittin' on the Dock of the Bay,* and offer a resource section including pointers on where to park if driving. There is much material out there if a reader cares to delve more deeply into local history, and I am indebted to authors of the area who have preceded me. I have done my best not to copy their labors but admit to extracting from them and bringing my own twist to things. I hope you enjoy!

Please keep in mind some of the locations of boats mentioned in the tours may change or they may simply be gone.

Chapter One

Sausalito Human History

The town's name is said to be derived from the Spanish word *saucito* meaning little willow. Apparently there were such groves in Sausalito in the early days which were an indicator for the nearby freshwater springs. Various past spellings for Sausalito include Saucelito, Sousolito, Sausilito etc.

The Miwok Indians

The Coast Miwok Indians inhabited Marin County including Sausalito for thousands of years prior to Spanish contact in the 16th century. They called this area Lewan Helowah or West Water, and were hunter-gatherers living in small groups without a centralized political authority.

The Miwoks lived in permanent villages the Spanish called rancherias. They also had seasonal hunting/fishing camps. They had several different types of shelters including dome-shaped homes with a willow branch frame covered in grass or Tule reeds. Another design incorporated a similar framework but with a redwood bark covering. These villages usually included a communal roundhouse for ceremonial dances and other activities, and a sweat lodge.

A Miwok staple was the acorn which they ground into a flour to make bread or a type of porridge. They also gathered mussels and clams, grasses, bulbs, berries and ate elk, deer, rabbit and birds. The Miwoks fished and were great basket makers. They believed in animal and human spirits and thought that the animal spirits were their ancestors.

Historical written records of the Miwoks start somewhere around 1579 from a priest on Sir Francis Drake's ship. The Spanish and the Russians also have accounts of the Miwoks.

In the early 1800s the Spanish missionaries moved the native peoples onto the missions and at the same time started dividing Marin-Sonoma into large ranches. In this manner the Indians were taken from their tribal lands and worked in servitude to many of the land grant owners. European diseases decimated the population. A smallpox epidemic struck around 1838. Pre-contact population was about 3,000, and their numbers were reduced to 60 by 1880.

The last full-blooded Miwok is said to be a man called Tom Smith who died in 1932 at the age of 72. Tribal status was not gained until 2000. The Federated Indians of Graton Rancheria (formerly Federated Coast Miwok) were finally recognized by the federal government. This included people of Southern Pomo and Coast Miwok lineage.

William Richardson

In 1822 William Richardson appeared on the scene. He sailed into San Francisco Bay as the first mate of the *Orion* and landed at Yerba Buena Cove (San Francisco). He married Maria Antonia Martinez, the daughter of the Commandant of the Presidio. They were married after he joined the Catholic Church and was baptized Don Antonio Richardson. He started off teaching carpentry, navigation and boat building at Mission Dolores. He was the Captain of the Port of San Francisco for a while.

In 1838 he received a 19,500 acre Mexican land grant called

Sausalito the early days circa 1908 with yachts and houseboats in Richardson's Bay. Angel Island in the far background with Belvedere's Peninsula Pt. upper left. Photo courtesy Sausalito Historical Society.

El Rancho del Sausalito covering all the land north of the Golden Gate Bridge up to Mt. Tamalpais. Don Antonio envisioned building an empire.

He sold vegetables, firewood and water to visiting ships, took in duties and port fees, and raised livestock. Unfortunately, he was unable to capitalize on the California Gold Rush which he thought would bring him prosperity. He imagined ships anchoring in Whaler's Cove in Sausalito to purchase supplies from his various enterprises but instead they anchored off Yerba Buena (San Francisco). The smaller groups of gold seekers that did come through Sausalito tramped through his land, stole cattle, squatted and moved on to the Sierra foothills. When they lowered Richardson into the ground on April 20, 1856 at age 61 he was broke. Supposedly he died from mercury poisoning from his medicine for rheumatism.

Old Town and New Town Sausalito

Samuel Throckmorton, a lawyer who had worked with Richardson gained control of most of Sausalito and sold it to a

1910 view north on Waterstreet (now Bridgeway) from Princess Street. Far left notice the Arch El Portal after which today's El Portal Street is named. Far right is the Sausalito Land & Ferry Co. office built in 1902. Upstairs was the first Sausalito public library circa 1906. Photo courtesy Sausalito Historical Society.

group of San Francisco businessmen in 1868. That group became the Sausalito Land and Ferry Company. They had surveys done, named streets after themselves and bought a ferry called the Princess after which Princess Street (downtown) is named. Basically, they owned most of the land in what is called New Town Sausalito, the portion of town which is north of Whaler's Cove (Old Town). Old Town is located just south of Sausalito's bronze waterfront Sea Lion sculpture. The cove here used to be a favored deep water anchorage for boats.

The Sausalito Land and Ferry Company officials proposed and executed various business schemes but they never amounted to much. Luck changed in 1871 when this company struck a deal with North Pacific Coast Railroad. Tracks were built down into Sausalito from the north. Now there was a good connection between north coast lumber and Yerba Buena (San Francisco), which also linked various communities and brought more commerce. New residents moved in with more opportunities to be had. Wealthy San Franciscans moved to the hills of Sausalito, and the workers lived along the waterfront.

Sausalito the early days at the train terminal. Engine #14 named the Tiburon. Photo courtesy the Sausalito Historical Society.

Old Town developed much more slowly and for many years was more or less cut off from the railroad and ferries that served New Town. Regardless, the first school in Sausalito was built here in 1869 on West Street. Today the original structure, completely remodeled is a private residence. In the 1870s new owners, controlling most of Old Town, incorporated into the Old Saucelito Land and Drydock Company, sold lots and started boat-related services. Major Orson C. Miller arrived and purchased all the unsold land and formed Sausalito Bay and Land Company, lining out the streets and linking Old Town to New Town. Yet Old Town remained somewhat stagnant and its main claim to fame is probably for its boat building and repair activities in the cove. Today there is one small grocery store, the Golden Gate Market, and a few other businesses amongst a primarily residential community. The sloping hills of Old Town drop steeply down to the waterfront cove, bringing at times intense offshore winds which gives this place the nickname "Hurricane Gulch."

In the 1880s Sausalito had a reputation as being a "racy" place and thus provided a destination for many San Franciscans out for a little adventure. Sausalito was an interesting community with its mix of British, French and Portuguese citizens, and the

Old Town Sausalito with Castle by the Sea (left) and Cottage by the Sea (now gone) at today's intersection of Bridgeway & Richardson Street. Photo courtesy the Sausalito Historical Society.

contrasting lifestyles of those who lived on the "hill" versus those camped along the waterfront. The pretty belles from San Francisco made their way to Sausalito for champagne parties on yachts.

In fact, Sausalito is considered to be home to the first yacht club on the West Coast. Actually the San Francisco Yacht Club had its roots in San Francisco's Mission Bay but soon moved to Sausalito. A split occurred between members, the old timers wanting to set up the clubhouse in the deeper and historic waters of Whaler's Cove (Old Town) and those choosing New Town. Sausalito ended up with two yacht clubs, the Pacific Yacht Club in Old Town and S.F. Yacht Club to the north. As the old members died off so did the Pacific Yacht Club. The San Francisco Yacht Club survived and was located in what is today Trident Restaurant overlooking the water. The club, however, moved to Belvedere Cove in 1927.

Around 1893 the town incorporated, in part to control development. It was a place that attracted free thinkers and artists as well as businessman. There's some history of brothels

San Francisco Yacht Club circa 1890 (front center). The three cottages to the right are Lolita, Lucretia and Lurline. Today there are just two left, and the S.F. Yacht Club is the Trident Restaurant. Photo courtesy the Sausalito Historical Society.

and gambling rooms, but this is generally overblown and in 1900 there were almost as many churches as saloons.

After the 1906 earthquake, Sausalito like so many other towns became a refuge for many San Francisco citizens. By 1910 the population was around 2,380. New Town developed with its ferryboat and railroad connections, bringing more commerce and supporting new shops and businesses. This is exactly how the Sausalito Land and Ferry Company owners envisioned things.

The Northwest Pacific Railroad in fact kept up passenger service here until 1941 and freight service until 1971. There are still a few places in Sausalito where you can see the old train tracks.

On January 16, 1920 the 18th Amendment to the Constitution outlawed making and distributing alcohol (repealed by the 21st Amendment December 5, 1933). Regardless, in the early 1920s it was relatively easy to purchase alcohol in Sausalito. Bootlegging became popular and Marin County with all its secluded waterways and beaches became a landing zone for rumrunners. Drivers like Baby Face Nelson (Chicago bank robber Lester Gillis) would then drive their trucks and automobiles loaded with illegal booze onto the Sausalito ferry bound for San Francisco. Because of the lack of funds to police the port and inspect vehicles, deliveries to the cities speakeasies were very successful.

Of course Sausalito got its fair share of illegal alcohol, and in town at the gaming parlors or at private residences it was easy to get a drink. The historic beer garden, the Walhalla, built in Old Town on Whaler's Cove was rumored to have a trap door leading to the beach below. Since the Walhalla was overlooking the water boats could easily pull up on the beach and deliver or receive bootlegged booze.

Marinship: The World War II Years

The Bay Area in general is well known as a center for ship building during World War II, while Southern California was a hub for the aircraft industry. In fact, the shipbuilding industry brought an influx of over 500,000 men and women to the area. By 1944 one-sixth of all wartime ship builders lived in the Bay Area. Ship construction occurred throughout the area in places like Mare Island, Richmond, Oakland, Hunter's Point and Sausalito.

Sausalito became an important shipbuilding town during World War II. The U.S Maritime commission authorized a shipbuilding center here, called Marinship, to supply ships for the war effort. W.A. Bechtel won the contract.

Starting in March of 1942, residents of the area called Pine Hill had to vacate their homes. Forty-two structures and homes were torn down or moved. The hill was leveled, and the dirt used to fill in and grade the land along the waterfront in the Marinship district (northern Sausalito). Two thousand workers toiled around the clock to prepare the 210 acre shipyard. Twenty-six thousand pilings were pounded into the mud to build six shipways, two outfitting docks, 21 buildings (workshops and warehouses) and a railroad track. A shipping channel also had to be dug out to get the big ships out of Richardson's Bay. A 1 ½ mile-long, 300 foot wide channel (3 million cubic yards of mud were dredged) was made.

They called in E.C. Panton, construction manager, and said, 'Ted build us a shipyard over in Sausalito. You'll find there's a big hill in the way, with thirty or forty houses on it, and there's a swamp, but don't let that bother you. And I almost forgot, there's a railroad switch-yard, complete with shops, warehouses and turntable, that will have to be cleared out of the way. Well, go to it Ted; don't rush but have it ready for a keel-laying in about three months.
-From *History of A Wartime Shipyard* by Richard Finnie

In fact, the first keel was laid four months after ground breaking while Marinship was still being constructed. Two months later the first ship was launched. Approximately 75,000 workers came to Marinship to work in shipbuilding and support industries during the war. This influx completely transformed Sausalito as well as the waterfront area known as Marinship. Over the course of 3 ½ years (1942-45) 93 vessels were built: 15 Liberty ships, 78 T-2 tankers (roughly every thirteen days a ship was constructed). Twenty-three vessels were repaired in Marinship as well. Marinship was a 24/7 building machine using an innovative north-south assembly line. Two ton slabs of steel plates were stacked at the northern end and were sent along the line being transformed at every stage into the parts needed for

Marinship WWII (upper center). Photo courtesy the Sausalito Historical Society.

the ships. The first ship launched was a Liberty ship, the William Richardson.

Marinship closed in May 1946. Soon the population of Sausalito dropped back to pre-war levels at around 3,500, and the town settled into a quiet period. Eventually Marinship began dismantling in 1950.

In that same year in Old Town, overlooking Whaler's Cove, the historic German restaurant and beer garden, the Walhalla, was re-opened by Sally Stanford under the new name Valhalla. Stanford was a colorful character. A former madam of a bordello in San Francisco, she eventually became mayor of Sausalito. The Valhalla over the years has changed ownership and names many a time.

In the '50s and '60s, half a dozen old ferries ended up on the shores of northern Sausalito. These unique living spaces attracted artists and those choosing to live a "different" lifestyle. The liveaboard ferries, and many other boats and barges converted into waterfront liveaboards, created issues of wastewater discharge and general pollution. There was a growing pressure to move those living the alternative waterfront lifestyle into established floating home communities. Today's Sausalito floating home community, eclectic and intriguing, is internationally known and has over 400 homes.

The floating home community has become more gentrified, and the waterfront in general has been cleaned up substantially. Sausalito's real estate is now amongst the most expensive in the world (residential housing averaging $1,258,000 in 2016). The resident population remains relatively small (7,061 as of the 2010 census) but downtown is packed with tourists on busy summer weekends. The beauty of the Sausalito hills, sometimes capped in fog, dropping down to Richardson's Bay and the vistas of Angel Island and San Francisco makes Sausalito as appealing and dynamic as ever.

Chapter Two

Belvedere, Tiburon & Angel Island

Included in this chapter are brief histories of Belvedere, Tiburon and Angel Island which can all be viewed across the water from different locations along the Sausalito waterfront.

Belvedere and Tiburon

Belvedere is a finger of land extending off the greater Tiburon Peninsula. The tip of this finger, pointed at San Francisco is called Peninsula Point.

Belvedere, or "beautiful view" has had at least six different names over the years, the current one dating back to the 1880s. Belvedere actually consists of Belvedere Island and Corinthian Island with Belvedere Lagoon (east side of Belvedere Island) between the two. The use of the word island is a bit confusing. Both these "islands" are attached to Tiburon (Spanish for shark) and each other by land. Historically, these strips of land connecting to Tiburon were just that, meaning that at high tides there did indeed appear to be two islands. However, over time these strips of land were filled in and widened, and the lagoon itself was largely filled in.

ANGEL ISLAND

Camp Reynolds

Belvedere
Peninsula Pt.

Raccoon Strait

14

Around Peninsula Point is Belvedere Cove, once home to the floating ark community of the late 1800s and where you'll find Corinthian Island.

Over the years Belvedere has been home to the Miwok Indians, Spanish vaqueros, forty-niners, the U.S. Army and a most influential resident, Israel Kashow.

In 1835 the Rancho Corte Madera del Presidio land grant was awarded to Irishman John Reed, including all the land of the Tiburon Peninsula extending to the shore. Belvedere Island became his portrero (pasture) because in those days it was almost an island with just a narrow isthmus connecting it to Tiburon. A fence was put across the isthmus and cattle and horses roamed the "island" without escaping.

The days of the large ranches began to end after the Bear Flag Revolt and the Americans took over California. An East Coast transplant named Israel Kashow discovered Belvedere and lived there for 30 years starting around 1855. He has been called a squatter but perhaps should more aptly be called an energetic man of commerce. He built a house for his family where today's San Francisco Yacht Club is located in Belvedere Cove. He raised sheep, cattle, planted fruit trees and ran a cod fish drying business, canning around 300 to 700 tons a year. He also bought about 139 acres of tidelands in the area.

But controversy never left. Whose land was it? Was Belvedere legally part of the Corte Madera del Presidio Rancho? (See *Sausalito Stories* chapter.) The first survey (1858) done by the Americans of the rancho did not mention it. Meanwhile Kashow remained and continued his various enterprises.

The U.S. Army had its eye on Belvedere, which they called Peninsula Island and claimed it was owned by the U.S. government. By 1871 Peninsula Island fell under the command of the Camp Reynolds (Angel Island) garrison. While the military placed a small command on Peninsula Island Kashow, with a little legal maneuvering, stayed on, finally receiving a lease from the Army.

Cod fishing became big business and at one point there were two cod fish drying stations on Belvedere. One as mentioned was run by Kashow (located near today's Beach Road in Belvedere Cove) who at times employed up to 100 Chinese workers. The other cod fishery (Pescada Landing) was built along the tidelands on the west side of Belvedere Island facing Sausalito in 1877. There was a large wharf, warehouse, living quarters, and drying racks. The cod fishing boats anchored in Richardson's Bay.

In the 1860s there were oyster beds off the northwest side of Belvedere. John Morgan ran Morgan Oyster Company, and in fact rented some of the tidewater areas owned by Kashow. There was an oyster bed off Belvedere and two off Strawberry Point. During certain times of year a sailboat called Pet made daily trips to San Francisco, delivering oysters. Morgan's company eventually moved operations to the South Bay in the early 1870s.

In the 1880s there was a ship demolition and salvage business in Belvedere Cove. At least 16 vessels were stripped and salvaged including the USS Monadnock, a Civil War monitor. The Monadnock deck was primarily made of iron, and had to be blasted apart with dynamite.

Eventually Kashow's reign on Belvedere ended, and in 1885 the courts ruled that Belvedere was part of the original Reed land grant. Kashow was evicted. Through certain legal maneuverings, the ownership of Belvedere fell into the hands of a group of businessmen who formed the Belvedere Land Company. Belvedere's name came from this time.

The land company immediately began planting trees (3,500) and the open bare hills of Belvedere, once the Reed portrero for grazing livestock, became transformed.

Over the years Belvedere was developed but strict city regulations on construction have helped maintain the idyll charm that has made it one of the most expensive communities in the world. Also restaurants and stores are not allowed on Belvedere Island.

After World War II the Belvedere lagoon was filled in even more and tract homes were erected. Bit by bit the lagoon and the spit of land called Beach Road (connection between Belvedere Island, Corinthian Island and downtown Tiburon) were further developed. As of the 2010 census the population of Belvedere was 2,068.

As mentioned before part of Tiburon's Peninsula extends behind (east) Belvedere, including downtown or Main Street overlooking the waterfront, and a ferry dock connecting passengers to Angel Island and San Francisco. This is also the past location for the southern terminus of the Northwest Pacific Railroad, bringing cargo and passengers to the ferry docks. The railroad stopped operating in 1967 and is now a residential complex.

Some of the largest old-time ferries operating on San Francisco Bay were in fact built in Tiburon boat yards. On the backside or eastern shoreline of the peninsula, a Navy coaling station was established in 1904 where Roosevelt's Great White Fleet once stopped for refueling. During World War II this coal station became the U.S. Navy Net Depot, making and servicing huge underwater nets meant to keep enemy submarines and torpedoes from entering San Francisco Bay. Currently, this location is the Romberg Center for Environmental Studies and is run by San Francisco State University.

Looking from Sausalito to Belvedere, if you follow the shoreline to the left, past a series of water level homes, Belvedere ends and the Tiburon Peninsula continues. Deep into the bay to the north is the Richardson's Bay Audubon Center and Sanctuary. It is here where the historic Lyford House (see Chapter Seven) now stands.

This area of Richardson's Bay is actually off limits (even to kayakers) from October 1 to March 31 as a dedicated wildlife sanctuary for migratory birds.

In this same general direction, look high up the hillsides to see open space, which is Ring Mountain, comprising 367 acres of Marin County parks land. Here long ago, the Coastal Miwok Indians chiseled petroglyphs on granite-like boulders. You will also find rare plants like the Tiburon Mariposa Lily unique to this park.

The 2010 census lists Tiburon's population at 8,962.

Angel Island

17

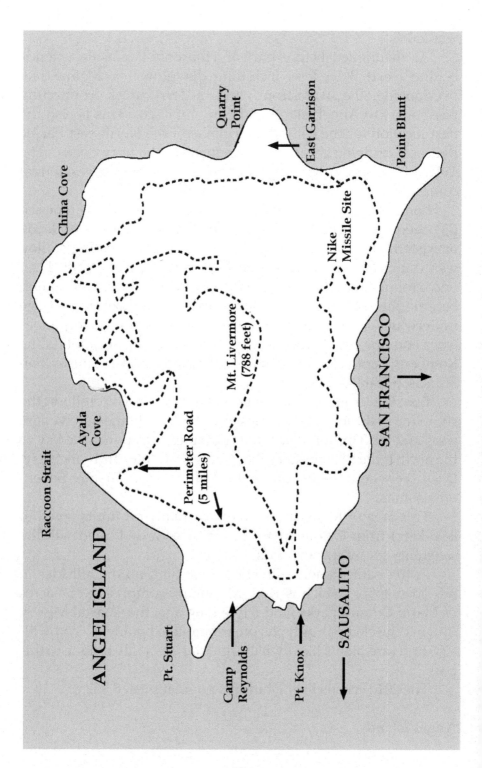

ANGEL ISLAND

Raccoon Strait

China Cove

Ayala Cove

Pt. Stuart

Camp Reynolds

Pt. Knox

Perimeter Road (5 miles)

Mt. Livermore (788 feet)

Quarry Point

East Garrison

Nike Missile Site

Point Blunt

SAN FRANCISCO

SAUSALITO

On the west side of the island, facing Sausalito, there is an open area with a cluster of historic buildings. This is Camp Reynolds dating back to the Civil War period. This is just one aspect to the fascinating history of Angel Island.

The Miwok Indians, long before the arrival of the Europeans, paddled their reed boats with double bladed oars across to the island. They established hunting villages, and artifacts dating up to a thousand years ago have been found on the island from five different sites.

Juan Manual de Ayala sailed into the Bay on the San Carlos in 1775 and anchored in Ayala Cove on Angel Island. His voyage followed a land based expedition in 1769 with Gaspar de Portola, credited with being the first Europeans to see the San Francisco Bay.

Captain Ayala's navigator, however, was the first to chart out the Bay. A period of time passed but in the early 1800s the Spanish began building the Presidio and the Mission Dolores over in what is today called San Francisco. The Spanish concern was to protect their interests in Alta California. At this time there were many outside influences they wished to defend against, and they believed they had rights to all of Alta California (today's California).

Beginning in the late 1820s American whalers sailed into the Bay anchoring at Whaler's Cove in Sausalito. The Russians, with their bases in Bodega Bay and Fort Ross hunted otter in the Bay and maintained a storage facility on Angel Island for their valuable pelts. Americans with native hunters from the Aleutian Island chain also encroached into the Bay hunting otter. Other foreign ships cruised the California coast with trade goods. There was much for the Spanish to be concerned about.

Earlier in 1814 the H.M.S. Racoon, a British war ship, came into Ayala Cove (formerly known as Racoon Bay, Hospital Cove etc.) on Angel Island for repairs. The H.M.S. Racoon had been sent to the Columbia River through the persuasions of the Northwest Fur Company (British) to remove an American outpost (Fort Astoria) interfering with their monopoly of the region. However, by time the warship arrived, the Americans had already sold the Fort to the Northwest Fur Company. The H.M.S. Racoon left, all onboard disappointed that they had taken no "war spoils," and promptly ran aground on the treacherous Columbia bar. The ship was severely damaged, and the men worked the water pumps day and night as they sailed south, until they eventually beached at Ayala Cove for repairs. The body of water between Angel Island and Belvedere/Tiburon is today called Raccoon Straits, a slight misspelling that has survived over the years.

Mexican independence from Spain occurred in 1821. In 1839 a land grant was awarded to Antonio Maria Osio for Angel Island. Over a number of years he populated the island with up to 500 head of cattle. Sausalito's famous land owner and resident, Captain William Richardson supplied some of the boats that brought the cattle over.

But just as the Bay Area in general was under a constant state of flux, so was Angel Island. In 1846 the Bear Flag Revolt occurred and the Mexicans were kicked out by the Americans, and in 1848 California was officially taken over by the U.S. government. Osio lost his rights to Angel Island and the U.S. government took over.

In the 1850s a group of Army and Navy officials met in San Francisco to discuss fortifications to protect the city and bay. Fortifications were built at Fort Point (south end of the Golden Gate Bridge) and on Alcatraz. At the outbreak of the Civil War officials felt more protection was needed and that artillery batteries should be built on Angel Island, among other places.

The Civil War army post, Camp Reynolds, which as mentioned can be seen from Sausalito was built starting in 1863. A row of officer quarters, a bake house, and a few other structures still stand today.

Just before that time on the east side of the island at what is known as Quarry Point, some of the stone mined was used on Alcatraz for fortifications. Rock from this quarry also went to help build the Mare Island Navy base in 1854, and in 1857 the California Bank in San Francisco. Some of the quarry materials were also used in the construction of Fort Point.

Camp Reynolds

In 1866 Camp Reynolds was vacated for a period and then later used as a recruitment post. There's an interesting story related to fortifications and batteries on Angel Island. The date was July 4, 1876, the centennial for American Independence. As part of the celebration, a barge was towed out into the middle of the Bay filled with explosives. The artillery battery at Point Knox (the first point southeast of Camp Reynolds) was to fire rounds at the barge to set it off, creating a huge explosive and fiery display. Thousands of people gathered along the San Francisco waterfront and other areas to watch the show. However, the rounds fired from the battery kept missing. Soon several navy ships took aim and also missed. Finally, to avoid embarrassment a boat was sent out to set off the barge. So much for coastal defense!

In 1891 Ayala Cove (where today ferries land with tourists ready to explore the island) became a quarantine station. Ships and passengers from overseas were quarantined to protect against the spread of infectious diseases. Ships were fumigated, all personal items were sent through fumigation stations on shore, and passengers were disinfected and quarantined if necessary. By 1907 the quarantine station had 47 buildings. Quarantine activities continued into the mid-'30s, and the base was considered surplus by 1946.

Meanwhile, just around a couple points to the east is China Cove, named after Chinese shrimpers who used the cove. China Cove between 1910 and 1946 became an immigration station. Many nationalities ended up being processed here, but the Chinese received the harshest regulations and restrictions. Upon arrival, whites were separated from other racial groups and the Chinese were isolated from the Japanese. Men and women were kept apart, including married couples. About 175,000 Chinese alone were processed at China Cove, sometimes waiting months as they had to prove family ties in the U.S. During World War I and World War II, enemy aliens were also held here. By 1946 there were about 50 buildings, while today around half a dozen remain.

From the years 1907 to 1946 Angel Island was also transformed into a major military processing center with the majority of the action occurring at the East Garrison of Fort McDowell near the old quarry. Recruits were trained and prepared to be sent to their posts. Soldiers coming back from the Pacific theater (Hawaii, Philippines, and Japanese islands) were processed for re-entry. Many of the large buildings still present today were constructed around 1910. This includes a 1,000 man barracks, a prison, a hospital, mess hall, officer quarters, administration buildings and more. The mess hall could seat 1,400 soldiers at once, and often for any given meal there were three shifts of diners. Between 1926 to 1938 about 22,000 soldiers were processed here per year, and towards the end of World War II the number far surpassed this (one year 55,000).

After the war the island was considered Army surplus. Marin County visionary Caroline Livermore helped get the island "State Historic Site" status. Soon acreage was purchased in Ayala Cove and became part of the California State Parks.

From 1954 to 1962 there was a Nike anti-aircraft missile site on the southeast side of the Angel Island near Point Blunt. This was actually just one of eleven such sites placed around the Bay Area during the Cold War. The radar station for the site was placed on the highest peak on the island then called Mt. Ida (today's Mount Caroline Livermore named for the ardent conservationist who spearheaded the campaign to create Angel Island State Park). The top was chopped off for a helicopter landing pad, and a manned 24 hour "ready station" along with all the radar equipment was set up there. Orders were relayed from a command post on top of Mt. Tamalpais. The Nike missiles had a range of 40 miles and soon enough became obsolete.

By 1963 after the Nike Missile site was decommissioned, the rest of the island with the exception of Point Blunt and Point Stuart (both remaining in the hands of the Coast Guard) became part of the Angel Island State Park. Since this time, when there were still approximately 253 existing buildings, more than half of these have been demolished, providing a little irony to the historic site status but returning the island to a more natural look.

In the late 1990s there was a massive eucalyptus eradication program in an effort to help nurture native species. More recently Mt. Livermore's peak, victim of the Cold War, was restored in 2002 with the dirt being bulldozed back up the hill, recontoured and reseeded. This raised the peak 16 feet for a total height of 788 feet. Today, standing on that lofty peak, one has stunning 360 degree views of the San Francisco Bay, four bridges and the surrounding lands.

Bay Area residents living here in 2008 might remember the devastating fire on October 12 that ended up torching 400 of the 740 acre island. Mt. Livermore was stripped bare but fire crews were able to stop the fire before it reached any of the historic buildings. The fire was so intense with 25-30 foot flames that it could be seen from Marin, San Francisco and the East Bay. The fire was started by a group of campers, adults and young girls adding wood to the charcoal only BBQ stands.

Chapter Three

Richardson's Bay-Natural History

Richardson's Bay has long played an integral part in Sausalito's history as a waterway for whaling ships, ferries, WWII vessels, colorful waterfront residences including the floating homes community, and as an important natural ecosystem.

It is named after the Englishman William Richardson and is surrounded by Sausalito, Mill Valley, Tiburon and Belvedere. (On many maps and other references you'll see Richardson Bay spelled without the apostrophe "s." However, originally it was spelled Richardson's Bay and some local experts say this is the correct spelling which is what I use in this book.)

Richardson's Bay (R.B.) is an offshoot of the greater San Francisco Bay, which is a large dynamic estuary fed with saltwater through the narrow opening of the Golden Gate. In addition, fresh water runs into the S.F. Bay from various rivers and creeks. Two-thirds of the S.F. Bay is less than 18 feet in depth, and a third of the Bay's original footprint has been filled in. Hydraulic mining from the 1849 Gold Rush was responsible for much of the "fill in" as silt and rock flowed from the rivers into the Bay. Eighty percent of the wetlands (tidal) are now gone.

The S.F. Bay and its outreaches, like the California Coast, experience two high and two low tides per 24 hour cycle. These are known as semi-diurnal tides because the daily high tides are unequal as are the low tides. The most extreme highs and lows come during the new moon (no moon) and full moon phases. These are called spring tides. In between, when the tidal ranges are the least is called neap tides. This in-and-out flush of water creates a dynamic and still vibrant estuary.

Despite its urban surroundings, Richardson's Bay is considered one of the most pristine estuaries on the Pacific Coast. This richness comes from a relatively large and undisturbed intertidal zone along with massive eel grass communities which support a large array of plant and animal life.

The outer boundary of Richardson's Bay runs approximately from Peninsula Point at the tip of Belvedere across to downtown Sausalito. Here the water depths run around 20 feet. Just past this, the water quickly drops to as deep as 100 feet. However, the average depth of Richardson's Bay at lower low mean tide is 5 feet. Tidal fluctuations run roughly between 4.5-7.1 feet.

Richardson's Bay is known as a "no discharge" area, meaning that nothing can be dumped into the water. This is an attempt to help protect a fragile and diverse environment including: rich fishery and mollusk populations, marine mammals and bird life. The main sources of pollution threatening R.B. are runoff from the land (including chemicals, oil, sedimentation, erosion), untreated wastewater (i.e. from boats, anchor outs etc.), treated wastewater from municipal sewage treatment plants and dredging materials.

As mentioned before the backbone to Richardson's Bay's relatively healthy ecosystem is the large eelgrass beds. There are also large areas of pickleweed. In the intertidal zone the tidal marshes of R.B. perform a number of important duties, from generating oxygen, filtering/cleaning pollution, providing coverage for animals such as shorebirds and invertebrates and providing detritus (decayed material) for the lower rungs of the food chain.

Further up the shoreline around R.B. you'll find native

California grasses, and trees like the Coast live oak, toyon and California bay.

Overview of Wildlife in San Francisco Bay

Below you'll find a general picture of the types of wildlife living in San Francisco Bay. The main categories are divided into invertebrates, fish, mammals and birds. Most of this wildlife is also seen in Richardson's Bay. This section is followed by another one focusing specifically on Richardson's Bay wildlife.

Invertebrates

Invertebrates or animals without a backbone, actually comprise 97% of all animals on this planet, and they can be found in fresh or salt water, in the soil or on the land and even in the bodies of other critters.

There are many types of invertebrates in the muddy sediments (layers also known as benthos) of the Bay. Some live on top of the mud and some burrow into it. Each has its own particular adaptation for survival. Examples of what you'll find are sea squirts, tube worms, clams, mussels, crabs and snails.

Fish

A fish is defined as having a backbone, lives in the water, breathes through gills, has fins and is cold blooded (meaning a body temperature similar to its environment). Fish in the Bay are categorized as bottom, middle or top dwellers. Some examples of bottom dwellers are the California halibut and the leopard shark.

The California halibut blends in with its surroundings and can change colors. At birth this fish has two eyes placed opposite on its head but right away one eye migrates towards the other. Both eyes end up on the same side of the head, giving it better vision since one side of the body lays against the mud.

The leopard shark is gray with black spots and bars. Sharks

in general do not have bones, but instead the skeleton comes from cartilage (similar to the human nose). They have unusual vision. On the one hand they have weak eyesight yet they have a unique layer in their eye which allows them to spot prey in darkish conditions.

The Shiner surfperch inhabits the mid-zone. Surfperch have 2-3 faint yellow stripes on the sides and front positioned teeth for eating invertebrates and small fish.

One of the well-known top dwellers in the Bay is the jacksmelt. They are long silvery fish which eat small crustaceans and plankton near the surface. They bunch together in large masses when threatened.

Mammals

Mammals are warm-blooded, air breathing animals. The two main aquatic mammals found in the Bay are the California sea lion and the Harbor seal. Periodically harbor porpoises and whales such as the gray whale also wander into the Bay.

Birds

San Francisco Bay is along the Pacific Flyway and home to millions of migratory birds during the winter. Dozens of species also use the Bay (open water, marshlands and mudflats) year round.

Birds of the open water include many species of ducks, cormorants, grebes, gulls and brown pelicans. They dive for their prey either from the air or water. One of the marshland birds is the endangered California clapper rail. Along the mudflats you'll spot egrets, herons, avocets and sandpipers among others hunting for invertebrates and fish in the intertidal zone.

An interesting side note is the fact that every fall, roughly 25,000 birds of prey (raptors) cross from the Marin Headlands by the Golden Gate Bridge (shortest crossing over open water along the coast) to the San Francisco side on their southward migration.

Snowy Egret (left) and a Cormorant

Introduced Species

In the last 140 to 150 years, approximately 100 species of "non-native" aquatic invertebrates (for example: Chinese mitten crab, European green crab, Asian clam) have been introduced to the Bay. Most of these have been introduced by accident. A common cause of introduction, has come from the release of ship ballast waters in the Bay. These ships come from foreign countries and hence carry foreign species in their ballast water and attached in some cases to their hulls. This in turn impacts the native flora and fauna. Also, most of the fish living in the Bay/delta environment are also non-native. One example is the striped bass.

Richardson's Bay Wildlife (a partial list focusing on critters likely to be seen)

Fish

There are about 55 species of fish that come into R.B. The shallow bay is a good place for spawning fish as well as young fish. The Pacific herring come in December through February to spawn in shallow waters among the eel grass. Otherwise they spend their lives in the ocean.

The Herring fishery is the only commercial fishery in San Francisco Bay and Richardson's Bay. During the winter you can see the Herring fishing fleet working the waters in circular sweeping patterns at night just off downtown Sausalito. The fleet is based in Sausalito and is strictly regulated by the California Department of Fish and Game.

The Herring lay their eggs on just about anything, including dock pilings and even eelgrass. Herring and their eggs provide a food fest for harbor seals, California sea lions, gulls, sturgeon and other predators. After the surviving eggs hatch, the larvae eat plankton.

The Herring fishery is known for roe called kazumoko. The small roe eggs taken from inside the fish are exported to Japan. The rest of the herring is used for chicken feed and pet food. The herring fishermen look for mean tides (not extremes) on moonlit nights to set their nets. There is also a small fleet of boats that have permits to gather roe from kelp.

We also get sturgeon, striped bass, steelhead trout, shad, salmon, perch, sole, flounder and the always intriguing bat rays.

Mammals

Harbor seals maintain a year round presence in R.B. These seals are from 5 to 6 feet in length and can weigh up to 300 pounds. Generally they have spotted coats ranging from dark brown to silver-gray to black. In the bay you can find some harbor seals with a reddish coat color. It's thought that this might be caused by trace elements like iron and selenium from the water, or that some change has occurred to their hair follicles. The males are a bit larger than the females. Harbor seals have no external ear flaps, and small flippers force them to crawl on their stomach/ chest areas. However, because they make good use of their tail flippers, they are great at periscoping their heads out of the water.

Harbor seals are born in March to May and pups weigh about

30 pounds. Pups can swim within a few hours of birth, and can be seen riding on their mother's back. Pups are weaned in 4 weeks. Adult females mate/birth each year and may live 25 to 30 years.

The two major pupping sites in San Francisco Bay are the Castro Rocks under the San Rafael/Richmond Bridge and Mowry Slough in the South Bay.

Harbor seals divide time between land and water about 50/50. They can sleep in the water but usually haul out. They can dive down to 1,400 feet and last approximately 40 minutes. However, most dives are much shorter, 3 to 7 minutes and not very deep as is the case in the relatively shallow area of Richardson's Bay. Food varies, ranging from sole, herring, octopus, flounder, hake, cod and squid.

Harbor seals are very sensitive to disturbance. A 100 yard comfort zone is recommended by the National Marine Fisheries. In Richardson's Bay this is often not possible, but a minimum of 30 yards should be maintained. If you see seals flush off their resting spot, you are too close. Seals need haul-out time to re-oxygenate their blood (for diving), to rest, to heal wounds, for the molting process and pupping.

California sea lions. The time of year we tend to see them in R.B. is during the winter herring run. Males grow up to 8 feet and a weight of over 600 pounds. They are tan in color but look darker when wet. California sea lions are larger than harbor seals and have external ear flaps. They also breed and birth on the land whereas harbor seals mate in the water.

The sea lion population is up since the passage of the Marine Mammal Protection Act in 1972.

Birds

R.B. has   been named an Important Bird Area (IBA). The Bay sees over a million migratory birds each winter. One of the first birds to show up is the solitary loon, soon to be followed by others. The mudflats of Bothin Marsh (west of Richardson's Bay Bridge and Hwy 101) is home to many of these birds. Also found in Bothin Marsh is the year-round endangered species, the Clapper Rail. R.B. has also been designated a Hemispheric Reserve of the Western Shorebird Network. Migratory shorebirds wintering here are the "Western sandpiper, Spotted sandpiper, American avocet, Dunlin, Marbled godwit, Greater yellowlegs, Willet, Long-Billed curlew and dowitcher."

During the winter it's not unusual to see large rafts of

Brown Pelican

Blue Heron. Photo-Patrick Davis

cormorants, smaller groups of buffleheads, western grebes and other water birds.

Certain months of the year you'll see our beloved brown pelicans that often migrate down to Baja for the winter.

Year round residents are the "great blue heron, snowy egret, great egret, black crowned night heron, mallards, red-tailed hawk, turkey vulture, killdeer, western gull, morning dove, rock dove, Anna's hummingbird, scrub jay, american crow, chestnut backed chickadee, common bushtit, bewick's wren, house sparrow, red-winged blackbird, house finch, song sparrow, and California towhee."

Rules of the Road

Please be respectful to wildlife. It is a gift to us all to be able to observe and enjoy wildlife so close to an urban setting. When birds fly off or seals scatter from their resting spot into the water, you are too close.

From October 1 through March 30, the Richardson's Bay Wildlife Sanctuary (owned and managed by the Richardson's Bay Audubon Center and Sanctuary) is off-limits to everyone including powerboats, sailboats, kayaks and swimmers. This 900 acre sanctuary provides an excellent refuge for wildlife especially during the winter migration period. The off-limits sanctuary is located between Strawberry Point (Mill Valley) running a line across to Tiburon and all the water north/northwest of this line. A series of white buoys mark the beginning of the sanctuary. There is one narrow boating channel in this area where boaters are allowed, and that is directly along the eastern shoreline of Strawberry Point.

The Audubon society was also part of a cooperative effort which started a native oyster restoration project within the sanctuary in 2004. The idea was to help create habitat to encourage native oysters to reclaim ancestral grounds. Before siltation from Gold Rush era mining, development and over-harvesting decimated the native oyster population, the S.F. Bay's oyster beds were prolific.

Oysters are great water filterers. In a single hour one oyster can filter out pollutants from up to 30 quarts of seawater. They also provide food for crabs, fish, bat rays, birds and humans. Currently there are a number of oyster research projects going on.

Chapter Four

Floating Homes and Anchor-outs

The waterfront lifestyle and specifically living on the water has played an interesting and sometimes contentious role in the history of Sausalito.

Floating homes (sometimes called houseboats) have existed on Richardson's Bay for over 100 years in one form or the other. This history of floating homes and liveaboards in Sausalito is related to what some say was the first liveaboard community on San Francisco Bay.

In 1890 various vessels began to anchor in Belvedere Cove. These vessels were used as weekend retreats, duck-hunting cabins and so forth by citizens of San Francisco. The type of liveaboard vessels that became prevalent in the cove were called arks. These second homes on barges or flat-bottomed scow hulls usually had a galley, four rooms and vaulted roofs. Families and friends spent time in their arks during the summer months. There were a range of merchants serving these floating homes, bringing wood, food, water and taking away garbage in small rowboats.

During the summer months in the 1890s there was an annual festival called "Night in Venice." Lights would be strung up on the arks, yachts and homes in Belvedere Cove for a night of music

Belvedere Cove arks late 1800s. Belvedere Lagoon in the background separated by today's Beach Road. Left Belvedere Island. Photo courtesy Belvedere-Tiburon Landmark Society.

and fireworks.

In the early 1900s there were about 35 to 40 arks in the cove during the summer time. They were towed into Belvedere lagoon for the winters.

In the aftermath of the San Francisco earthquake of 1906 many families took up long term residence in their arks, in some

Belvedere Cove early 1900s. Corinthian Island (then known as Valentine's Island) in the background, a floating ark and ladies rowing. Photo courtesy Belvedere-Tiburon Landmark Society.

cases beaching them on shore or setting them up on pilings.

Today you can see historic examples of these arks in Tiburon, at Sausalito's Ark Row, in Sausalito's floating homes community, and the maritime museum at Hyde Street Pier in San Francisco.

Sausalito's current established floating homes community was more directly born out of events related to World War II. During the war there was an influx of about 500,000 men and women to the Bay Area drawn to jobs in the booming shipbuilding industries and supporting sectors. About 20,000 of these workers were based in Sausalito as part of the ship building operations in Marinship. Naturally, housing was hard to come by, and some workers began living in boats and other structures along the waterfront.

When the shipyards along the Sausalito waterfront started closing at the end of the war there were a lot of surplus boats. Don Arques, whose father owned waterfront property, began buying up these surplus boats including barges, ferries and other types of floating vessels. He anchored these by the shore along his father's property. These surplus boats became homes for many bohemians from the '50s and later hippies from the '60s. Ferries became houses, and barges had homes built up on them. There were no rules along the mudflats in this unregulated environment-an anarchist's delight.

Floating Homes Community with Mt. Tamalpais in background

Anchor-outs on Richardson's Bay

Eventually these residents clashed with the law. The conflict peaked in the '70s and is documented in the film, *The Last Free Ride*. The issues were waste discharge and illegal residences. (See *Sausalito Stories*.) The resolution was to start establishing the legally sanctioned floating homes community which today Sausalito is famous for.

The established legal floating homes communities (there are five floating homes marinas with over 400 homes total) are not to be confused with the anchor-out community. It is illegal to anchor in Richardson's Bay for more than 72 hours in a given week without a permit. Anchoring longer requires one (good for 30 days max). Extensions can be granted by the Harbor Master presuming there is no intention to make permanent residence in R.B.

Currently there are large numbers of people living the anchor-out lifestyle without permits. This provides for an ongoing controversy. At issue is the discharge of blackwater and graywater into a no-discharge area, and it is just as illegal to anchor a home on public waters as it is to build a hut somewhere within the Golden Gate National Recreational Area. Anchor-outs are required to have a holding tank for all waste disposed of via honey barge service or to use a land-based pump out facility.

Involved in dealing with the historic and ongoing controversy

The anchor-out lifestyle. Best view in the house with Mt. Tamalpais in the background.

regarding anchor-outs are the Joint Powers comprised of the county of Marin, the surrounding cities to R.B. (Sausalito, Mill Valley, Tiburon, Belvedere) and the Bay Conservation and Development Commission (BCDC). The BCDC was formed in response to McAteer-Petris Act of 1965 passed to "regulate uses of the Bay" because of concerns over wastewater discharge, bay fill and navigational hazards. The BCDC is a state agency responsible for designing long-range plans for the Bay as well as overseeing any development affecting its waters.

State law says that a vessel anchored in one place for extended periods is considered "a type of bay fill." In part, this is because a permanent or semi-permanent anchor-out type boat/house just like artificial landfill can have adverse impacts on bay ecology. One impact is called "crop circles," when an anchor-out swings around on its anchor line which in turn mows down the eelgrass (critical habitat for herring to lay their eggs, for fish to hide and spawn, and the base of the food chain). Also, over the years many anchor-out vessels have sunk becoming navigational hazards as well as polluting Richardson's Bay. Who cleans up the mess? Certainly not the anchor-outs. Their ship goes down in a winter storm and no one cries out "abandon ship" faster. Eventually it is the tax payer that pays!

Shortly after its formation, the BCDC helped establish "private floating home" marinas or communities. Anchor-outs and people living in the tidal regions were given a chance to become part of these communities. They had to bring their homes up to code and berth them on the floating home docks. Many anchor-outs fought against this bringing on the houseboats wars of the 1970s mentioned earlier.

In 1985 the BCDC and the Joint Powers formed a plan to prohibit new anchor-outs, and also mandated the removal of existing anchor-outs. The Richardson's Bay Regional Agency was established that year to implement/oversee this plan. The process has been a slow one because of the long established history of anchor-outs along the waterfront community. Therefore progress is questionable. "In a 2008 survey RBRA counted 98 vessels in the anchorage. Between 2008 and 2014, RBRA abated 484 derelict or abandoned vessels. Nonetheless, in 2014 there were 205 vessels in the anchorage, a 209% increase over 2008." There was a jump in numbers as of 2016 to around 240 vessels. As of early 2017 after winter storms sunk many anchor-outs (which in turn had to be removed from the Bay), the number hovered around 200.

The Joint Powers that participate in the RBRA have had their controversies. One of which is the differing amounts they each pay into the RBRA to support its mandate. The county pays the largest percentage followed by the City of Sausalito. At the same time Sausalito also spends its own funds dealing with anchor out issues due to its frustration with the lack of action on the part of the RBRA. Because the city didn't feel it was getting its money's worth they withdrew from the RBRA as of July 1, 2017.

Besides the floating homes and anchor-out community, there are also those living aboard boats docked at various marinas. There are five main marinas with over 2,000 recreational boat berths. The no-discharge law also applies to these boat owners. Some marinas allow no liveaboards but end up having "sneakaboards," while others supposedly allow 10% of boats to be lived in. The rules are not entirely clear.

Chapter Five

South Sausalito Tour

In 1981 the Sausalito City Council established the Historic Preservation District. The main function was to protect the historic character of downtown Sausalito especially in respect to various buildings dating from the 1890s to the mid-1950s. Because of this vision, Sausalito today retains much of its historic charm.

The nexus of this historic district in downtown Sausalito is at the intersection of Princess Street and Bridgeway Blvd. This is the junction envisioned by the old Sausalito Land & Ferry Company (circa 1868) to be the center of the business district.

Princess Street is the epicenter of downtown Sausalito and is easily accessible. Therefore I've chosen to spotlight this street, and its many historic buildings. Some of the listed buildings are currently in use as commercial enterprises and a few as residences. Below I've identified them by street address followed by brief descriptions of their historical significance. Please respect the privacy of residences and simply enjoy them from the street view.

Start at Princess Street & Bridgeway.

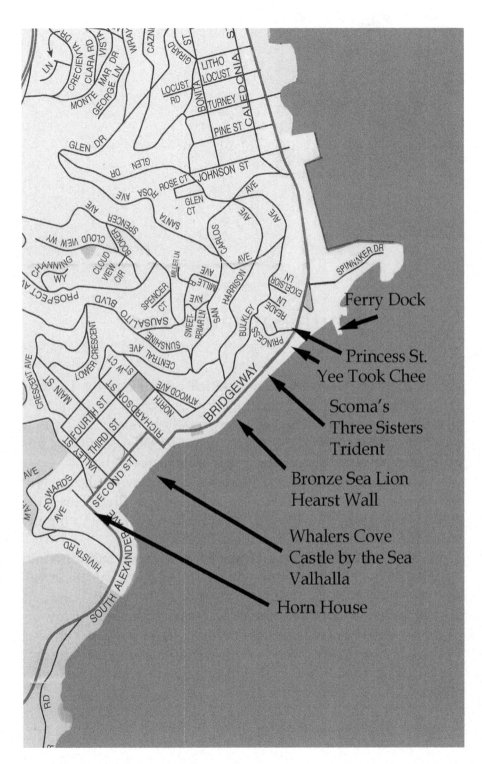

Ferry Dock

Princess St.
Yee Took Chee

Scoma's
Three Sisters
Trident

Bronze Sea Lion
Hearst Wall

Whalers Cove
Castle by the Sea
Valhalla

Horn House

4 Princess Street — Built in 1878

This three story building was originally Jacob Schnell's boarding house and saloon. It was conveniently built near the old ferry landing (now Yee Tock Chee Park) in 1878. The upper two floors still retain the original flavor and design of the building, however the first level, renovated over the years to accommodate retail outlets has lost its historic charm. (The third floor was actually added in 1890.)

19 Princess Street — Built in 1874

19 & 21 Princess Street

According to maps from the late 1800s this gabled roofed one-story cottage along with some of it's neighbors housed businesses involved in coal, wood and hay. You'll notice a couple large windows on each side of the front door. Originally these windows were much smaller.

21 Princess Street — Built circa 1887

This building could almost be the twin of 19 Princess Street. Also, a one story cottage with a gabled roof it was originally a private residence. It is virtually unchanged from the early days.

52 Princess Street — Built in 1894

This 1 ½ story cottage is another gem found on Princess Street and is purported to be more or less in original form. It has shiplap siding (overlapping wooden boards) and a lovely veranda which gives it a ranch-style feel.

Originally this was the home of Christopher "Charlie" Becker born in St. Louis, Missouri. Eventually he moved to California and settled in Sausalito in 1893. At that time there were only about 15-20 houses in town. He had various occupations over the years including: working on freight scows, as a ferryboat

pilot, engineer, brakeman, fireman, railroad conductor and town mayor (1904-1908). He had a small sign in front of his house that read: *Klein aber mein* (small but mine).

Charlie built the Becker Building (666 Bridgeway) in 1894. The first floor was a cigar and stationary shop with offices above. He was a popular figure in town and included amongst his friends, William Randolph Hearst.

62 Princess Street — Built in 1869

The builder was John Schoobert. The architecture includes a gable roof and Gothic-revival elements. It is said this was Sausalito's first hotel (Sausalito Hotel), and in the early days catered to shipyard employees and travelers. Later, this building became the town hall in 1904 and then in 1920 a Christian Science

church for 47 years. It is now the Gables Inn.

83 Princess Street — Built in 1884

This private residence, a Greek revival style cottage with its Tuscan columns on the veranda is a statement in charm. You can follow Princess Street up to Bulkley and go left for an overhead

perspective of this cottage. The house was built by John Richards, a real estate investor and also on the first Board of Trustees for Sausalito in 1893. (Note: This 1,901 sq. ft. home on .25 acre lot sold for 875k in 1988, and as of spring 2017 was valued at 2.1 million dollars!)

90 Princess Street — Built in 1897

Currently divided into private residences this bungalow style structure was built by George Urquhart. He lived upstairs and his paint shop was on the lower level. Future generations of Urquhart's continued to live here until 1967. According to the National Register of Historic Places listing, it has a "colonial revival veranda with Tuscan columns."

Note: There's another very interesting historical landmark at the end of Princess Street where it meets Bulkley Avenue. Just to the left across the street you'll see what are called "portals of the nook," an architectural reflection of an earlier time. These are the two fabulous arches spanning off a central column with an Iconic capital made from brick. Behind this entryway, and built in 1891 there used to be a Queen Ann shingle type house designed by the architect Willis Polk. Unfortunately it was taken down in 1961 and all that remains are the brick arches incorporated into a more modern structure backed by condos.

Yee Tock Chee Park-south of Princess Street & Bridgeway on the Bay side.

This is the original site of the first Sausalito-San Francisco ferry terminal. In 1868 the Sausalito Land and Ferry Company purchased the paddle-wheel steamer called the Princess (after which Princess Street is named). This was to provide convenient transportation for San Franciscans who purchased real estate in

Sausalito which back then was considered a country retreat.

In 1875 the North Pacific Coast Railroad (NPCR) established the first train service to Sausalito and the ferry terminal was moved more or less to its current location where the train tracks ended. However, in 1922 in response to a demand for an auto ferry, the Golden Gate Ferry Company began operating one at the old Princess Street location. Soon the NPCR now the Northwestern Pacific Railroad also began a competing auto ferry service to San Francisco from its location.

Yee Tock Chee aka Willie Yee after whom the park was re-named in 1975 (after his death) was a well-known and popular resident of Sausalito. Born in 1912 in China Yee came to the U.S. in 1912. Between the 1920s-1998 the Yee family ran a grocery store, the Marin Fruit Co. (605 Bridgeway) across the street from the park. The patriarch of this family was Willie Yee who was an active community member known for giving loans, credit and free deliveries. In 1998 surviving family members were forced to close down the business due to a huge spike in the rent.

Scoma's-588 Bridgeway

You'll find Scoma's just south of Yee Tock Chee Park on the water. Scoma's, although not in its original form, dates back to 1907. Originally it was situated a short ways to the north along

the waterfront but moved to its current location in 1926. Many different businesses have been run out of what is now a restaurant from bait shop to bar to restaurant.

Between 1907 and 1937, Mathias Lange ran Lange's Launch Company here. Lange was a well-known and hardworking Sausalito resident. His gas powered launches carried customers to San Francisco, towed sailboats, and ran fishing trips. Lange also sold bait, crab, and made sandwiches for boating parties. He served as the steward and custodian for the San Francisco Yacht

Club, his neighbor on the waterfront (today the former yacht club is the Trident Restaurant, adjacent to Scoma's).

The Three Sisters-579 Bridgeway

Located just across the street from Scoma's. There are actually only two sisters now, but originally the three sisters were Queen Anne style rental cottages built (1886) by Captain Charles Chittenden. They were constructed right next to each other with gabled roofs. The Three Sisters were named Lolita, Lucretia, and Lurline but in 1914 Lurline was torn down to make room for Sausalito's new telephone exchange. You can actually see where they cut away Lurline from her sisters.

The Trident-558 Bridgeway

This structure dates back to 1898. In those days it was the San Francisco Yacht Club. There was another building here prior to 1898, also the San Francisco Yacht Club but that burned down. It was in this earlier building in 1893 that papers were signed incorporating the town of Sausalito. The Trident building has a colorful past being owned by the Kingston Trio (folk and pop music from the '50s and '60s) at one point, and was included in scenes from Woody Allen's *Play It Again Sam* and various commercials

Bronze Sea Lion with Angel Island in the background, Raccoon Strait to the left and Peninsula Pt., Belvedere

including for Folgers coffee. Today it is a restaurant.

The Bronze Sea lion

Just south of the Trident along the waterfront just offshore, you'll see the bronze sea lion.

It was designed by Al Sybrian, who used to draw sketches of sea lions in this area back in the 1950s. His first sculpture (1955) was created out of haydite and concrete, but eight years of tides and currents took their toll. Due to the sculpture's popularity funds were generated and the original sculpture was replaced with today's bronze sculpture in 1966. But on New Year's Day in 2004 the 1,900lb statue was toppled off its perch by a wave. Shortly after it was repaired and returned to its base.

The Hearst Wall-475 Bridgeway

The famous newspaperman William Randolph Hearst lived for awhile on the hill across from the bronze sea lion. It was in this area that he considered building a great "castle." In 1890 construction began on a massive retaining wall with a central arch to support the gatehouse for his castle. The project ended here. At this time he had a mistress, Tessie Powers, living with him and it is said that the "local matrons" were offended by this. Hearst become an unwelcome resident and apparently was asked to leave Sausalito, and thus Hearst Castle was built in San Simeon, California instead. (See *Sausalito Stories*.)

Today if you look upslope of 475 Bridgeway you can see the central arch. Above it rests the front of a house built (1950) by architect Joe Esherick for Tom and Sybil Wiper who purchased the property from Hearst. (Please note: There is no public access to reach the Hearst Wall.)

Whaler's Cove and Nunes Brothers Boatyard

Shortly past the sea lion sculpture the straightaway of Bridgeway ends and the road takes a sharp right, turning into Richardson Street. At the end of Bridgeway go straight (on foot or bike) rather than taking the right turn and you'll see the boardwalk running above a shallow beach. You are now at Whaler's Cove. Take a walk along the boardwalk and enjoy the magnificent views.

Whaler's Cove, also known as the "cove" is located at the foot of Old Town Sausalito. Historically, this cove has been a popular anchorage for boats because of the deeper water, protected beach and easy access to water and firewood. Long ago freshwater streams and springs were abundant in this area, and the water came down the hills filling various watering holes. This water in turn attracted much wildlife including elk, deer, mountain lions and even some grizzlies. It provided the Miwoks with a consistent source of water as well.

In the 1820s ships began anchoring here to collect firewood and take on what was known as some of the "sweetest" water. Recognizing this potential after he settled in Sausalito, William Richardson started a business selling water, and later built a cistern to hold the "watery gold."

Richardson also worked on boats here in the cove, and the U.S. Navy did the same in the 1850s. Over the years various boat building and repair companies in turn set up shop. One of the

best known was the Nunes Brothers Boat and Way Company (1925-1960). The Nunes brothers originally came from the Azores and they were well respected sail and power boat builders. You can still see some of the old pilings in the water holding the ship ways and docks from the historic boat building days.

Castle by the Sea-on the boardwalk

This intriguing looking home is the first house you see at the

beginning of the boardwalk. It is easy to distinguish with its two turrets and was built in 1902. There used to be a one story saloon off its front level. The writer Jack London landed in Old Town Sausalito in the late 1890s, and there is some debate about where he stayed. Some say he stayed in the Castle by the Sea and others claim it was next door (to the right and across Richardson Street) at the Cottage by the Sea (now gone) where he rented a room. Regardless, it is believed London wrote some of his classic novel The Sea Wolf while staying in Sausalito.

The Walhalla, the Valhalla, Charthouse, the Antidote and so on

There's a large historic building with a long row of windows facing the water at the southern end of the boardwalk. In 1893 the Walhalla beer garden and restaurant was built. Over the years it changed hands and names, becoming one restaurant after another. In 1950 former San Francisco bordello owner Sally Stanford bought and renovated the Walhalla, changing the name to the Valhalla. Sanford became a well-known character and was elected mayor in 1976. She decorated her restaurant with Tiffany lamps, thick carpets and offered live piano music. She died in 1982. Since those days this location has been a Charthouse, an eatery called Antidote and Gaylord's Indian Restaurant. (As of February 2017 this space remains unoccupied and the city is reviewing a 20-unit condo complex proposal for this site which hopefully will retain elements of the basic historical structure.)

The Walhalla was one of the locations in Orson Welles' film *The Lady from Shanghai* filmed in 1947. Welles starred in it along with Rita Hayworth. In the movie there's a short of Welles and Hayworth standing on the boardwalk.

The Horn House-215 South Street

On the west side of the Valhalla find Second Street and walk left a couple blocks to South Street. You'll find this beautiful historic Victorian style home with its wrap-around porch. It has redwood siding, rooms with high ceilings and lots of ornate touches. Though it's difficult to view with all the surrounding foliage you'll be looking at probably the oldest surviving residence in Sausalito circa 1865. Part of the original house was actually shipped around Cape Horn. (Please note there is some debate about the exact date the Horn House was built.)

Chapter Six

Central Sausalito Tour

Start at Princess Street and Bridgeway. From here walk one block north to El Portal and take a right. Or if you are getting off the ferry go left to the first cluster of buildings and you'll see the hotel.

Hotel Sausalito—16 El Portal & Bridgeway

Located just south of the ferry dock this Mission-Revival style hotel was constructed in 1915. It's considered a boutique hotel.

The hotel has a colorful past some of which is verifiable and some that isn't. Early in the hotel's history it was rumored to be a bordello. Being close to the water and the terminus of the railroad tracks the hotel attracted sailors, railroad employees and artists. Later, during Prohibition the gangster and bootlegger Baby Face Nelson was said to have stayed here. During the 60s and 70s writers and artists like Sterling Hayden lived there along with other artists and beatnik generation personalities.

Some of the scenes from the movies *Partners In Crime*, *Serial*, *Mother* (Albert Brooks, Debbie Reynolds) were shot at this

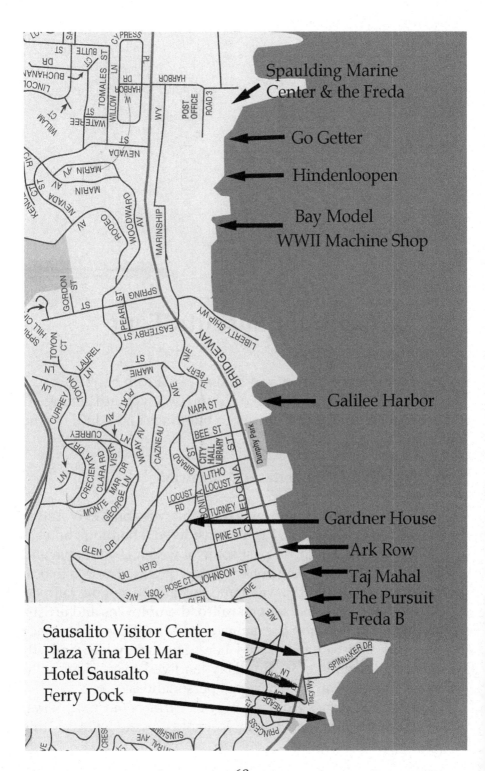

Spaulding Marine
Center & the Freda

Go Getter

Hindenloopen

Bay Model
WWII Machine Shop

Galilee Harbor

Gardner House

Ark Row

Taj Mahal

The Pursuit

Freda B

Sausalito Visitor Center
Plaza Vina Del Mar
Hotel Sausalto
Ferry Dock

location. The hotel underwent an extensive renovation in 1996.

Plaza Vina Del Mar — Bridgeway & El Portal Street

The park is just across the street from the Hotel Sausalito. The name comes from one of Sausalito's sister cities in Chile. It's a charming little place with landscaping (including Canary Island date palms) that combines Victorian elegance with a Mediterranean flair, historic sculptures and a War memorial.

Prior to 1904 this park was known as "the Pond." It was a stagnant watery bog full of garbage with a pungent odor. The Pond, then owned by the North Shore railroad, after years of complaints was filled in and deeded to the city in 1904 to become a public park. It was named Depot Park. Improvements were made over the years.

The first thing a visitor sees at the park's entrance, are a pair of matching elephants. The elephants along with the park's fountain were originally part of the Panama-Pacific International Exposition of 1915 in San Francisco. The fair celebrated the opening of the Panama Canal but also served to let the world know San Francisco was thriving after the 1906 earthquake.

William B. Faville designed the Court of the Universe which

included the elephants and the fountain as part of the 1915 fair. After the fair he shipped the elephants and the fountain to Sausalito where he lived. Since the construction of the Beaux Arts style buildings and sculptures of the fair were not intended to last the two elephants and the fountain were renovated in the mid-1930s. In fact a mold was made of one of the elephants, and became the two identical cement elephants we see today. Back when they first arrived the local children gave them the names Pee-Wee and Jumbo.

The park also has a war memorial originally dedicated to fallen soldiers of WWI. The memorial was moved in 1977 to its

current location just north of the park entrance and re-dedicated to those who died in all wars.

During the hippie years in the 1960s the park was closed because of large gatherings and the resulting trash (the park remained closed until 1996). In 1971 the park's name was changed to Plaza Vina Del Mar.

Casa Madrona Hotel-801 Bridgeway

This historic hotel was first built in 1885 by William Barrett, Secretary-Treasurer of San Francisco Gas and Electric Company as a home. In 1906 it was sold to John Patrick Gallagher who transformed it into the Casa Madrona Hotel. The original building, today seen up on the hillside above Bridgeway was referred to as *The Mansion*.

During WWII the hotel was used to lodge military families and after the war fell into disrepair and became a favorite "crash pad" for some members of the beatnik generation. The Deschamp family took over in 1956 and renovated the hotel. In 1967 Pink Floyd stayed here during their first U.S. tour. The room they stayed in was later named the Piper Room after their recently released album-*The Piper at the Gates of Dawn*. They were also photographed at the hotel for promotional purposes. One of the more famous shots being of the group lined up on the hotel's fire escape.

Sausalito Visitor Center & Historical Exhibit-780 Bridgeway (Aka the Ice House)

This historic building was originally a 1890s Northwest Pacific Railroad cold cargo hold that ended up in Sausalito in the 1920s. Around that time the Ice House was moved to Caledonia and Litho Street to hold and sell ice. In 1999 the Ice House was moved to its current location, and is now a visitor's center and

a one room Sausalito history museum. This is a must see stop while touring Sausalito for an easy, quick and interesting perspective on local history.

From The Ice House follow Bay Street towards the water. Look for the wooden boardwalk to your left (runs parallel to Bridgeway) which takes you along the Sausalito Yacht Harbor. Note: If instead you continue to go straight following Bay Street as it runs into a parking lot you'll see another boardwalk designated as Public Shoreline. Walk to the end to find a small charming pier extending over the water offering nice views of Richardson's Bay and across the way-Belvedere. This boardwalk ends up on the left side of the Spinnaker Restaurant.

Freda B-Sausalito Yacht Harbor Berth 907

I've included this boat because it's a beautiful replica of a classic 1860s coastal schooner. She was built in 1991 and is 80 feet long. She is called a "gaff-rigged topsail coastal schooner." The mainmast is taller than the foremast. The multiple sail set-up gives it speed and agility. The typical schooner like the Freda B has two masts but some were built with up to four masts.

Similar sailing vessels were first used by the Dutch in either the 16th or 17th century. Later the design evolved in North America in the early 1800s, and really came into fruition in the 1900s in New England. These tall ships or schooners had many uses as ocean voyagers or making coastal runs. They were used heavily by the merchant trade but also for hauling slaves, outrunning blockades, and privateering.

Formerly an East Coast charter vessel, the Fred B was brought to California in 2010, and is a charter boat owned by S.F. Bay Adventures.

The Pursuit-Sausalito Yacht Harbor Berth 910

The Pursuit is an 82' old classic known as a M Class sloop with sleek and beautiful lines and a long history of winning big time races. It's laid out with Mahogany planks over steel frames. In 1937 it was brought out to the West coast and current owner, Ron MacAnnan purchased her in Los Angeles in 1960. MacAnnan an engineer and contractor by trade was a command gunner on B-29s during WWII.

His love for classic boats extended well beyond the Pursuit. Since 1933 the Galilee, had been resting in the Sausalito mud and slowly deteriorating. In 1975 MacAnnan led the charge to save a part of this historic brigantine sloop. He took a chain saw and cut off a 20' section which today you can view at Fort Mason in San Francisco.

MacAnnan is considered a Sausalito Legend with a personality at times cantankerous but also gentle and friendly. Now in his 90s most likely you'll see him driving around town in his white 1949 pickup truck or making repairs on his beloved Pursuit.

You can continue walking northward along the boardwalk

to see the next two sights. First you'll come to A Dock for the Taj Mahal, and then continue to Johnson Street and Bridgeway for Ark Row.

Taj Mahal-Pelican Yacht Harbor-A Dock

This floating home is hard to miss although it pales in comparison to the original Taj Mahal built in India in the 17th century. That Taj Mahal (Crown Palace) is considered one of the eight wonders of the world and is a physical expression of love and passion. Muslim Indian ruler, Shah Jahan, built the Taj in memory of his beloved wife who died after giving birth to their fourteenth child. The Taj was built entirely of white marble and is a mausoleum housing both their bodies.

Sausalito's Taj Mahal has its own mystique, a unique looking floating home, geometric in design like the original Taj, at its best perhaps at night with its moody interior light glowing out onto Richardson's Bay. This floating home, based on Islamic inspired architecture, has been here for about 40 years.

Building the Taj was started by Prentice Hale, retail magnate and owner of San Francisco's once famous Emporium. The cement barge for the Taj was built by Forbes Kiddoo in 1968. Kiddoo was credited with developing "full height" ferro-cement hull barges for floating homes, the type of which you see now supporting

most of these homes. Some local residents might remember Forbes Island built by and lived in by Kiddoo, anchored in Richardson's Bay. Forbes Island is now located by Pier 39 in San Francisco.

In the mid-70s developer William Harlan bought the Taj and finished the project. There are three levels, 12 rooms to this 4,500 sq. ft. home that looks like something from the *Arabian Nights* stories. The Taj is a mix of Mughal and Moorish architecture with Islamic, Persian and Indian influences. It is a fascinating blend of "arabesques, ogee arches, cupolas and colonnades." It is easy to recognize with its twin onion-shaped domes.

Inside there are two kitchens, two master suites, an upper level solarium for meditating, a sauna, a secret elevator, marble floors, mirrored walls and a wine cellar. Since Harlan's days there have been several owners of the Taj and various renovations.

Ark Row-Corner of Johnson Street & Bridgeway

Go back to the boardwalk and walk north to find Johnston Street.

Ark Row is a series of historic arks on pilings along the shoreline. (For more on Ark history see Chapter Four.) You'll see the Midway (1929), the R.Flower (built 1915, restored 1987), the Bohemian (1918), The J.H. Madden (1936) and #515. Next is the Julie Marlowe built in 1914 and restored in 1988.

The Madden was owned at one time by a former mayor of Sausalito who did time for his involvement in the alcohol trade during prohibition. Later, he was re-elected for another term. The Midway, more or less in its original condition, has the distinction of being only one of two arks that still has its wooden hull. It is also the last ark to be constructed on the Bay.

The Gardner House-47 Girard Avenue

Follow Bridgeway north 1-2 blocks and go left on Turney Street and up three blocks to Girard Avenue.

I've included this house not only because it is one of the oldest (built 1869) and relatively un-altered houses in Sausalito but also because it is an absolute gem. The house was built on one of the earliest lots sold by the Sausalito Land & Ferry Company.

The builder and first resident was James H. Gardner, a former Senator from South Carolina. He spent time in the Sierra gold mines before coming to San Francisco and investing in real estate. Later he moved to Sausalito.

Galilee Harbor-300 Napa Street

To get here locate Bridgeway and Napa Street. At this intersection go towards the bay on Napa and you'll see Galilee. You can walk the docks and enjoy this eclectic collection of floating homes and liveaboard boats all part of the Galilee Harbor Community Association.

Galilee is a cooperative community open to maritime workers and artists as part of an effort to preserve the working waterfront of Sausalito.

Galilee has a colorful history as a maritime waterfront community. Back in the 1880s Italian fishermen built traditional sailing vessels called *feluccas* here. In 1906 San Francisco citizens,

who had vacation homes on this waterfront, moved in when their city residences were destroyed. In 1936 the Galilee dropped anchor here and during Sausalito's World War II shipbuilding period, barges were constructed on this site. Later in 1957, Cass Gridley started a fish processing facility, a fish market and a restaurant serving fish and chips. During

the 1960s to '70s the community was full of colorful liveaboard vessels, and boat building industries continued. Residents began to organize in 1978 to protect their waterfront lifestyle and after tortuous years of applying for permits and litigation, in 2003 the current community's docks were completed and tenants moved into the Galilee cooperative.

You can walk these docks or loop around them by kayak. We call this the *Pirates of the Caribbean* tour. On the northern side of these liveaboard homes you'll see a marshy area (between Galilee and Schoonmaker Point Marina) with coyote and tulie grass, representative of the more typical shoreline prior to development. Here you can also see the skeleton of the Galilee at low tide, interned forever in the mud.

The Galilee has an interesting history. She was built in Benicia, California, in 1891 at the Matthew Turner boatyard. She was a 180 foot brigantine and is said to hold the fastest time for a commercial sailing vessel crossing from San Francisco to Tahiti (22 days, a record that still stands). She was a sleek speed machine. Eventually, the Galilee was beached in Sausalito (1933) at Galilee Harbor, and was a liveaboard for 42 years. As mentioned earlier in this chapter the chopped off stern ended up at Fort Mason in San Francisco. The bow was cut off in 1987, and can be seen at the Benicia Historical Museum.

Turner's shipyards (initially in San Francisco's Mission

Bay area and then Benicia) from 1864 to 1907 churned out 228 vessels, and Turner is credited as being the most "prolific sailing shipbuilder" in American history.

Stationed onshore at the foot of the Galilee docks are two pilot houses that came from the Issaquah ferry. The Issaquah was built in 1914 in Washington State. She was a 114 foot two-decker steamer running trips on Lake Washington. In 1918 she was brought down here and was in service until 1948.

Just like the Vallejo and the City of Seattle ferries she was divided into living spaces. She was anchored on the mudflats in what is today the floating homes community at the north end of Sausalito. By the early 1970s she was in serious disrepair and eventually only a few parts were salvaged, including the pilot houses at Galilee.

The Bay Model — 2100 Bridgeway

The official address is misleading. The Bay Model is not found on Bridgeway but down below. Find the intersection of Bridgeway and Marinship Way (across the street from the 7-11 store). Go down the hill and continue straight. Follow the signs to the Bay Model and the parking lot. From here walk along the water to the right and you are at the Bay Model.

These warehouses, home to the Bay Model, date back to 1942 during the Marinship era. At that time the Bay Model was called the Warehouse and was built to store "outfitting materials and general stores" for the ships. After the basic structure of the ships were built in the ship ways just north of the Bay Model they were towed and tied up at the two long docks (since rebuilt) you can see today waterside of the Bay Model. It was here that all the outfitting took place including anchors, engines, boilers and all furnishings. You might notice how high these two docks are above the water. They were built to be at the level of the ships decks for easy on/off.

Undoubtedly, the most significant fact in this history is that ninety per cent of the men and women who worked at Marinship had never

worked in a shipyard before...not a single one of our ships ever had a major structural or a major power failure. -R.L. Hamilton, Production Manager

At the peak of production nearly forty percent of all welders were women, and they could 'burn rod' with the best of the men. -Marcia L. Patterson, Women's Counselor

In these historic buildings, a model of the San Francisco Bay and Delta region was constructed in 1957. One reason for the construction of the model was that in the 1940s John Reber, a local theater producer, devised the Reber Plan to build two dams in the Bay to create freshwater reservoirs. The dams were

to be built where the San Rafael Richmond and Bay Bridges are today. Congress allotted $2.5 million to study the proposal. The Bay Model, at a cost of $400,000, was constructed to run tests to help determine the validity of the Reber Plan. Reber died in 1960 before the tests were finished in 1963 which proved his plan unfeasible.

The Bay Model is maintained by the U.S. Army Corps of Engineers and is approximately 2 football fields in size. The model replicates the Bay and delta estuary and watershed. From 1958-2000 the model was used for scientific research by simulating currents and monitoring sediment movement, as well as testing for pollution patterns such as oil spills. The purpose of the Bay Model has now shifted from research to educational facility, with many interesting and informative displays about the Bay environment. Also there is the fascinating Marinship Exhibit covering Sausalito's WWII shipbuilding era.

Along the shore just north of the Bay Model you'll see a large pile of garbage. This actually comes from the Bay. The Army Corps of Engineers is responsible for picking up flotsam and jetsam floating in the Bay that poses a hazard to the shipping channels. The Raccoon, an Army Corps boat (one of several) is berthed at the Bay Model dock, built with a long crane for picking up debris.

The Raccoon was originally a Navy aircraft recovery boat dating back to World War II. The Army Corps of Engineers purchased the Raccoon from Navy surplus in 1959. They added the pilot house and crane along with a few other modifications. (See *Sausalito Stories* to read how the collection of floating hazards on the Bay began.)

WWII Machine Shop Building — 25 Libertyship Way

As you exit the Bay Model building walk along the waterfront to the right. Shortly this will bring you to a side street and you'll see the massive Machine Shop building to the right.

This 27,500 square foot machine shop was built in 1942 in the area known as Marinship. Here machinists and associated workers toiled 24-7 in three different shifts. Many of the workers here were black, and in fact black women. Both of which were of consequence in terms of breaking down the barriers to integration for blacks and women. Within this machine shop workers fashioned parts for the Libertyships and T-2 Tankers built in Marinship along the waterfront.

Post WWII Marinship was transferred to the U.S. Army Corp of Engineers. In 1950 the machine shop building was converted for geotechnical testing. In the early 1990s an "analytical laboratory" was put in. Since 1997 the building has been unused. The U.S. Department of Veterans Affairs took over the building in 2006. They were looking for a tenant to take over this space, and considered tearing down the structure and rebuilding a new complex in its place. This would be the cheaper option.

A 2010 V.A. report indicated a new foundation and seismic upgrades alone would cost $13 million. Regardless, many members of the Sausalito City Council, considering the historical significance have advocated over the years for the building to be saved. But the V.A. as a federal agency is exempt from local zoning and development regulations.

However, as of early 2017 it looks like the V.A. will preserve this building, which is now listed as a local and National Historic Landmark. Exactly when and how the building will be renovated

and who the future tenant will be are questions still to be answered.

The Hindenloopen-Marina Plaza Harbor

The easiest way to find this beautiful old boat is by walking from the Bay Model parking lot. Go north following a sidewalk by a playing field. Then go right and find the Marina Plaza Harbor home to the Modern Sailing Club. It's a short walk. The Hindenloopen is on the furthest dock in this marina to the left at the very end. If you must drive get back on Bridgeway and go north three signals and right on Harbor. Then an immediate right on Marinship Way following this to a stop sign. Go straight and the road turns to Testa Street at the end of which is the marina.

This uniquely shaped Dutch canal boat was built in 1905 in Belgium. The black hull is made of iron pieces riveted together. The Hindenloopen, which translates to the "galloping deer," helped evacuate soldiers from Dunkirk beach during World War II.

The Go Getter and Arques Marina. Located at Sausalito Shipyard & Marina-Harbor Drive & Road 3

Find Harbor Drive (off Bridgeway) and go towards the bay. Look for Road 3 after Mollie Stones supermarket and the U.S. Post Office. Right on Road 3 and proceed through the gate into the Sausalito Shipyard & Marina. Immediately to the left you can walk out on the first dock and find the Go Getter on an outside slip. (Note: Entrance to this dock is now via a locked marina gate. If you're lucky it might be open or you'll see someone opening it who won't mind you sauntering down the dock for a closer look at the old tugboat.)

The Go Getter is docked at what is historically well-known as the Arques Marina (now Sausalito Shipyard & Marina). This marina has significance for several reasons. It is the part of Marinship where the Liberty ships, tankers and oilers where put together during World War II. Arques is also home to the Arques School of Traditional Boat Building as well as to various ship builders that make small wooden boats. This is really the only place where wooden boats are still built in Sausalito. Finally, this is where many floating homes are constructed and restored by Aqua Maison.

The Go Getter was built in 1923 in Houghton, Washington. She was an ocean-going tug hauling lumber from Seattle to Los Angeles. The entire boat is made of Douglas Fir. The Go Getter is infamous for being a strike breaker brought into San Francisco Bay when Crowley Maritime's tugboats were on strike. She was

decommissioned in the early 1970s. The Go Getter is a lovingly restored liveaboard now, brought over by its current owner from Oakland many years ago. Sometimes at night, drifting by in a kayak, you can see a shadowy figure in the back deck's moody light playing a mandolin.

Spaulding Marine Center (Spaulding Boatworks & Arques School of Traditional Boatbuilding)-600 Gate 5 Road

Two ways to find this place. At the end of Road 3 just before you enter the Sausalito Shipyard & Marina there's an alleyway to the left where you'll find the Spaulding center. Or find Harbor Drive and Gate 5 Road next to the ICB building and go south on Gate 5 Road.

If you love classic wooden boats this is the place to check out. It is a Sausalito gem. You can take a free self-guided tour, see boatbuilding in process, and run across tools that are more than 100 years old like the Camelback Drill Press. Plus the historic boat, the Freda is berthed here.

Myron Spaulding was born in 1905 in Eureka California. His family moved to San Francisco when he was a boy where he later earned a credential in boatbuilding and naval architecture. This was the beginning of a long love affair with wooden boatbuilding which led him to become a very influential and respected craftsman. He was the designer/builder of the Clipper Class and the Spaulding 33 amongst other boats. Myron was also a racer and captained the *Dorade* to win the 1936 Trans-Pac race to Hawaii.

During WWII in Sausalito he helped build subchasers. He was also a violinist and played for the San Francisco Symphony until 1957.

In 1951 Spaulding bought the boatworks property in Sausalito. The Spaulding Marine Center is a non-profit business with a mission to connect people to the area's maritime history of boat building. Spaulding died in 2000 and his wife followed in 2002 but she left a trust in his honor to fund the center and

78

continue his work.

The center (20,000 sq. ft.) has a working boatyard and is home to the Arques School of Traditional Boatbuilding. The school was initiated with an endowment from Donlon Arques before his death in 1993. The non-profit's mission in Arques' words:

A school and center for the restoration of small wooden boats that have had historical significance in the greater San Francisco Bay Area.

Freda-Located at the Spaulding Marine Center

The Freda is arguably the oldest sailboat on the West Coast. She's a graceful looking centerboard sloop of the type immortalized by the French impressionist painters, Manet, Renoir and Monet. These artists themselves were sailors and the American sloop had a heavy influence on French boat design at the time.

The Freda is also of historical significance since she was built locally in 1885 on Beach Road in Belvedere Cove. She was named after the daughter of the first owner, Harry Cookson a saloonkeeper. Designed for sailing and racing on the S.F. Bay this gaff rigged sloop has a 32 foot long deck and is 52 feet overall. In 2004 the Freda was rescued from the mud in San Rafael and restored by the Arques School of Traditional Boatbuilding, and is

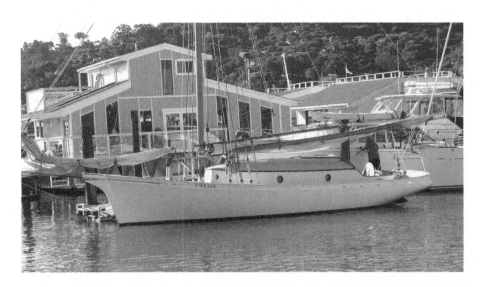

owned by the Spaulding Wooden Boat Center. She was completely rebuilt with new timbers and planks along with a reconstructed main cabin. In May 2014 the Freda was re-launched. (Note: Both the Arques School and the Spaulding Wooden Boat Center are also located at Sausalito Shipyard & Marina.)

I stood entranced for a long time, absorbing her poised loveliness as if she were mine to kidnap and sail away towards those dream harbors. -Ernest Gann writing about the Freda for *Rudder Magazine* April 1970.

Chapter Seven

North Sausalito Tour

Industrial Center Building (ICB) — 480 Gate Five Road

From Bridgeway take Harbor Drive towards the bay passing Mollie Stones market and the U.S. Post Office. Soon you'll see the massive ICB building on the left.

The ICB is a historic structure built in 1942 in what is known as Marinship, the center of local ship building during WWII. Back then this building was called the "Mold Loft and Yard Office." The first floor housed administration offices, and was also used to make templates and for storage of tools. The second floor was the "engineering and production departments," and the third floor was the Mold Loft. Here they made the molds which were used to fabricate parts for the ships.

In 1957 this 110,000 square foot building was purchased by Ernest and Polly Kettenhofen. They changed the name to the ICB. Initially they leased space for light industrial use which in turn evolved in artist studios. The ICB is now a three floor artist complex with about 100 artists. Every year there are several open studio events here.

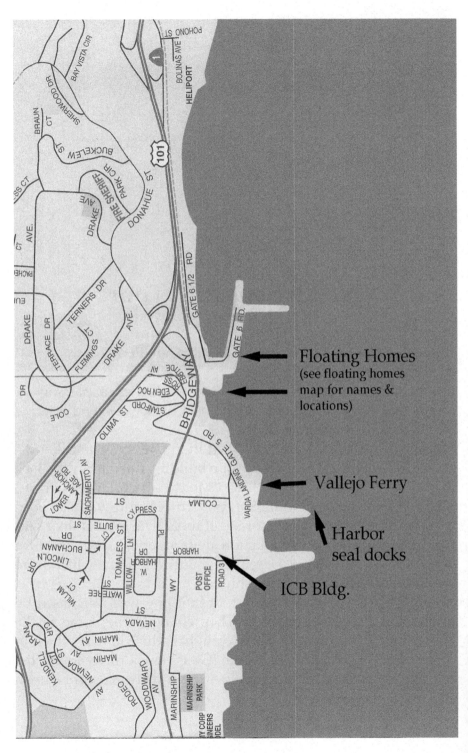

Floating Homes
(see floating homes map for names & locations)

Vallejo Ferry

Harbor seal docks

ICB Bldg.

The Harbor Seal Haul Out Docks

The primary location where Harbor seals haul out in Richardson's Bay is challenging to get to. But I'm including it because Harbor seals are the focal point of marine life here. And they are just so intriguing and fun to watch. If you have just stopped to check out the ICB building afterwards continue towards the bay on Harbor Drive. You'll come to the huge parking lot of Clipper Marina. Drive into this and go left all the way to the end. Here there is a parking lot that runs out on a spit of land. At the tip you can see the perimeter of Clipper Marina which is lined with pilings with logs lashed in between which acts as a sort of breakwater. Here you can see seals hauled out. At certain times of day and year it is not unusual to see 70 or more. The marina docks are accessed by locked gate but if you can catch someone entering Basin 3 or 4 and walk out to the end of the docks you can get a closer look at the seals. Of course the best way to see the seals here as well as catch them swimming in the bay is via kayak or stand up paddleboard.

There are not many haul out sites left in the South Bay

region where seals can get out of the water to rest. Please give these fascinating creatures space. The law says that you cannot approach closer than 100 yards. In reality, this busy urban environment challenges the likelihood that one can maintain this great a distance. Sailboats and powerboats leaving the marina pass within yards of the seals as the boats head for the main channel. Small boaters like kayakers should try to keep at least 30 yards away. When the seals start paying attention to you, rolling their leery heads as well as maybe jumping back in the water, you are too close.

Ferryboats of Sausalito: The Final Resting Place

During the '50s and '60s six ferryboats ended up along the shores of Sausalito. Once queens of the Bay, the era of bridges and autos ended their reign. Nonetheless, they are a rich part of the Bay's maritime history and fortunately some of that history has been preserved. The Vallejo and the City of Seattle can still be viewed along the northern waterfront today. Another ferry, the Berkeley, was bought by the City of San Diego and was restored. She was towed out the gate in 1973, and Sausalito lost an opportunity to keep a rich piece of history. The Berkeley was built in 1898 in San Francisco and was the first propeller-driven and steeled hulled ferry built in the city. Over her 61 years of ferry service she carried millions of passengers between San Francisco and Oakland. In 1906, the Berkeley was used to evacuate people from earthquake torn San Francisco.

The other three ferries met a more tragic fate. The Charles Van Damme in its last years was a restaurant located at Gate 6 Road (northern Sausalito) but eventually fell apart. The City of San Rafael was wrecked, the Issaquah crumbled, and today all that remains are the two pilot houses at Galilee Harbor.

The Vallejo Ferry-20 Varda Landing Road

From the ICB building follow Gate 5 Road north past the Anchor Cafe to Varda Landing. Follow the road along the right side of the 18-22 Varda Landing building to the bay and you'll see the Vallejo. (Warning: This whole area floods during winter storms colluding with high tides.)

Interestingly, there are two different versions of where the Vallejo was built. One story claims the ferry was built on the East Coast in 1871 and powered around Cape Horn to the West Coast. The other claims she was built in Portland, Oregon, in 1879. Regardless, the Vallejo was built with an iron hull.

In 1923 Robert Rauhauge, who ran the Mare Island Line, took ownership. Eventually his son became the skipper and the Vallejo was taken out of service in 1947. On the Mare Island run the ferry sometimes carried 1500 passengers and up to 2,000 when they packed them in. The fare was 5 cents.

In 1947 the Vallejo was sold for scrap to a steel mill in Oakland. She was brought to the Arques shipyard in Sausalito to be dismantled. The rebirth of the Vallejo started at this point. Three men, the artists Jean Varda and Gordon Onslow-Ford, and architect Forest Wright were looking for a large studio. They

bought the Vallejo and towed it to a spot on the Sausalito waterfront. Soon Wright left, and there were just two owners, Onslow-Ford and Varda.

They scavenged among the abundant materials found along the waterfront, many leftover from the war and customized the Vallejo. It was a tradition along the waterfront not to pay for things. And they painted the smokestack yellow, which is still its color today.

Varda, nicknamed Yanko, was a colorful character in personality and dress. He painted his car purple. He wore a green shoe on one foot and a yellow shoe on the other. He was an excellent cook and presided over lavish luncheons from his large straw chair telling stories. The wine flowed, and there were always plenty of women.

The two artists worked at their creative endeavors in the morning. Onslow-Ford painted, and Varda worked away at his colorful collages. Other tenants moved in and out, and there was always time for partying. The Vallejo in many respects was the center of the local art scene, and it represented a freedom of lifestyle soon to disappear.

In 1961, Onslow-Ford leased his side of the ferry to the philosopher Alan Watts. Alan Watts brought together eastern and western philosophies, and is one of the authors of the humanistic movement that led to the era of consciousness raising in the '60s. He was a Buddhist scholar and wrote books, taught seminars, explored sensory awareness, the human potential and more.

Watts and Yanko cut a door between their apartments for easy access, and Watts soon became a co-host at Yanko's revered lunches. Once again the Vallejo was a cultural center for spiritual and artistic pursuits, and in many ways the soul of the floating homes community during the '60s and '70s.

In 1967, an interesting gathering of counter-culture heroes

met on the Vallejo and held "The Houseboat Summit." Included were: Alan Watts, Timothy Leary, Allen Ginsberg and Gary Snyder. Their discussions ranged from dropping out to "taking over" the system. To read a partial transcript from this meeting see the *Sausalito Stories* chapter.

Varda died in 1970, killed by a street thug in Mexico and Watts died in 1973 while sleeping on board the Vallejo. Some say Watts "went on an astral trip and never came back."

Marion Saltzman, a friend of Yanko's, moved into his space. Watts had given his ownership up to the Society for Comparative Philosophy. Since then there have been several owners, and more recently the Vallejo underwent extensive restoration including being hauled out to patch up the hull. It is privately owned and is a liveaboard.

The Floating Homes Community

The floating homes community has been an interesting part of Sausalito waterfront history. These unique homes are tied up to central docks and have all the modern services: sewage, electricity, phone lines and cable. Over the years the community has been gentrified as new owners bought old funky floating homes (often converted boats) to get a slip, junked it, and brought in modern expensive homes. A floating home owner today pays a hefty slip fee much like home owners association fees for condos as well as a mortgage. The definition of a floating home in tax terms has changed, and owners can now deduct mortgages from their taxes. Most floating homes rest on cement hull barges instead of the foam blocks of yesteryear. (See Sausalito Stories.) The cement hulls are long lasting, and necessary if you plan on financing your purchase through a bank.

When walking the docks of the floating homes community please be very respective of the residents privacy by keeping voices down and obviously don't knock on anyones door. For those on a bike if you can't lock your bikes in the parking lot please walk them while exploring the docks.

You can actually start this tour either on the south or north

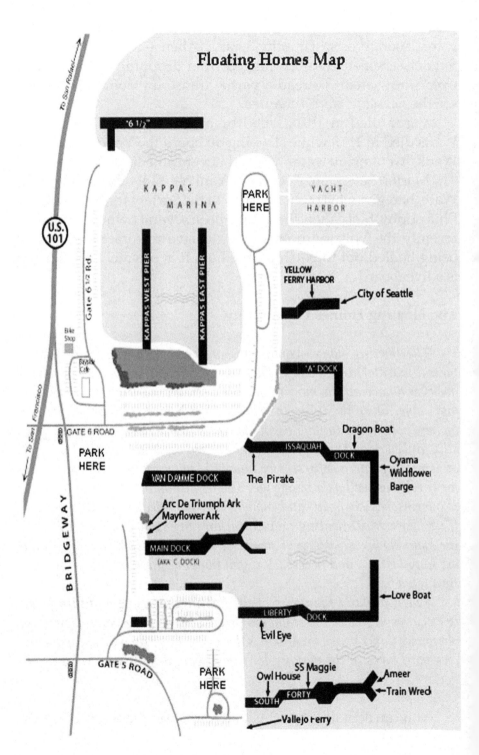

Floating Homes Map

end of the main community. If driving it is best to just park your car and do a walking tour of the various docks. If you want to start after visiting the Vallejo Ferry get back on Gate 5 Road and almost immediately you'll take a right at 245 Gate 5 Road turning towards the bay and park if driving. You can also start at the north end (find Bridgeway and Gate 6 Road and park). I've listed some of the more interesting floating homes starting from the southern end of the community. Make sure and check out the floating homes map to get your bearings.

The Owl- 43 South Forty Pier

This floating home is hard to miss as it towers above the surrounding homes. It gets its name because the top floor is shaped like an owl's head with two windows forming the eyes. It was designed by Chris Roberts and I've read different reports claiming it was built in the '60s and another saying the '70s. Regardless, the design, materials and the building of The Owl were fueled by the psychedelic era. The basic form of The Owl took shape around a tall tower-like structure that one author called an old pile driver and another an "old wooden stiff-leg crane."

SS Maggie- 34 South Forty Pier

Built in 1889 as a steam schooner to carry light cargo, she was retired in 1939 and became a home. The different levels of this floating home add up to about 2,500 square feet of living space, and she was extensively restored in the 1990s. Below decks you can still see parts of the original hull (Douglas fir on an oak frame) integrated into a more modern interior design. The SS Maggie, however, still retains a nautical vibe with wooden steering wheels, portholes and other nautical devices.

Train Wreck- 23 South Forty Pier

Construction started in 1976. The builder integrated an 1889

North Pacific Railway Pullman train car into the design, which was chopped in half. There are three levels, two bedrooms and two bathrooms. The middle level has the Pullman car dining room with its original brass fixtures and mahogany paneling. The dining room is surrounded by a modern living room boasting art from around the world. There's also a den/tv room. Downstairs is the master suite with a Jacuzzi. The top level is an eagle's nest study with lots of Bhutanese and Indonesian artifacts. Train Wreck is 1900 square feet.

Ameer- 25 South Forty Pier

The Ameer was built in 1910. Phil Frank, the well-known cartoonist (San Francisco Chronicle comic strip "Farley") and historian lived here from 1973-85 and is responsible for many of the renovations. There are four bedrooms and two bathrooms in this 2,000 square foot floating home.

The Evil Eye- 8 Liberty Dock

This home is on the south side of Liberty Dock fairly close to

shore. It was the home of Shel Silverstein (1930-1999) author of the ever popular books *The Giving Tree* and *Where the Sidewalk Ends*.

Silverstein was an author, poet, cartoonist and songwriter. In fact, he wrote the lyrics "A Boy Named Sue" for Johnny Cash, and "Sylvia's Mother" and "Cover of the Rolling Stones" for Dr. Hook & The Medicine Show. There's a great You Tube video with a recording of "Sylvia's Mother" on his floating home that not only brings you back to the funky '70s but also shows some interior shots of the home.

The Evil Eye, named after Silverstein's music publishing company and penchant for "staring down" people with one eye, is built up over a World War II balloon barge (see The Love Boat).

After Silverstein's death, his close friend Larry Moyer lived on the Evil Eye. Like Silverstein, Moyer known as the King of the Waterfront, was also a renaissance man. Moyer was a Universal Life minister, painter, actor, filmmaker and photographer. His bedroom and painting studio on the Evil Eye was called "The Tower," and literally hung over the water. Moyer also had a second studio, which was an anchor-out in Richardson's Bay, a short skiff ride from his floating home.

Both he and Silverstein at one point both worked for playboy magazine. Silverstein as a writer/cartoonist and Moyer as a photographer. Moyer died in February 2016, a great loss to the waterfront community and its ties to a more colorful past. As of

April 2017 the Evil Eye was for sale, empty and soulless waiting for hopefully yet another reincarnation.

Anchored offshore from Liberty and Issaquah Dock there are a handful of anchor-out homes that have been in place for years, and though illegal seem to be tolerated by officials. One of these is the Glass Barge, the floating art studio of Larry Moyer's who lived on the Evil Eye on Liberty Dock. The Glass Barge has been there since 1989. Next to this is the Phoenix or TeePee, a white teepee looking structure on a cement barge, originally built in the 1970s. The TeePee has been at its current location since 1988 and is a solar powered green living home. Northwest of this home is the Night Heron, built over an old World War II lifeboat hull with wind and solar energy systems.

The Love Boat- 52 Liberty Dock

Look for the round black hull (looks like a large lifeboat) and white upper structure. On the side of the barge you can read: *U.S. Army B.B. 1624*. This is a World War II balloon barge boat. This type of barge was towed into position, often in a harbor, to provide air defense against low flying enemy planes. Barrage balloons, used heavily by the British to protect cities like London, were released from the foredeck attached to steel cables. Once deployed, the cabled balloons created dangerous flying hazards, forcing planes to higher elevations.

The Love Boat was fitted on a cement hull in 1987. The hatch that released the balloons is a skylight for the master bedroom. There are two bedrooms, two bathrooms and a large open upstairs with kitchen, dining and sitting rooms.

Next you'll come to Main Dock where Otis Redding stayed and found the inspiration for his song Sittin' On The Dock Of The Bay. (See Sausalito Stories.)

North of Main Dock there are several homes extending offshore on pilings. Two of these homes are historic floating arks dating back to the early 1900s in Belvedere Cove (the Mayflower and the Ark de Triumph).

The Mayflower-Shoreside Just North Of Main Dock

The name plaque dates this home to 1907. Building actually started in 1906 but was put on hold because of the devastating earthquake in San Francisco that year. Apparently it was built as a wedding gift by a San Francisco businessman for his daughter. The Mayflower (1,200 square feet) with its 19th century Victorian motif was brought to its current location between 1920 to 1930. There is one bedroom and one bathroom. The interior still has its original redwood paneling, windows and doors. The bathroom light comes from portholes and there's a claw foot tub.

The Ark de Triumph- Shoreside Just North Of Main Dock

This is another historic ark, built, I believe in 1910 and pulled onshore after World War II. It is actually comprised of two arks attached together (end-to-end). I've read two different accounts of its origins. One that said this home was one of the original historic Arks from Belvedere Cove. Another story says it is rumored to have been living quarters for farm workers on the California Delta. Not long ago a recent owner ran a bed and

breakfast in this home.

Just north of the arks is the Van Damme Dock. This is actually the new dock for what used to be known as the Gates Cooperative. This cooperative was originally formed in 1979 and was recognized by the state. It used to be a "ragtag collection of houseboats" tied up to a series of rickety docks with overhead power lines strung along poles. Many of the residents had been living the bohemian waterfront lifestyle since the '70s, and represented an era characteristic of the waterfront during the formative years ('50s-'70s). Several years ago the cooperative was completely renovated and all the floating homes where moved to the Van Damme Dock. Though the Van Damme Dock now looks more like the surrounding floating homes community with its million dollar homes the residents living here are in subsidized housing.

The Pirate-4 Issaquah Dock

One of the earliest gas-powered tugs on the Bay in the 1930s this boat was built in 1910. It used to make the run between San

Francisco and the Sacramento River Delta. It has three levels. Below is the captain's bedroom, bath and sauna. The mid-level has an elegant dining room, galley, cozy bar, sitting room and outside deck. Upstairs is a master bedroom, bath and office.

The Oyama Wildflower Barge-61 Issaquah Dock

Wesley Oyama had this lavish home built in 1978 at the cost of a million dollars. There are three levels on this 4,000 square foot home. The upper level is designed in traditional Japanese architectural style and includes a tea room. Six carpenters were flown from Japan to create this environment. In contrast, in the lower level there is a high tech room with a large screen and surround sound system. There are two bedrooms and bathrooms and an indoor hot tub.

The Dragon Boat- 51 Issaquah Dock

This behemoth floating home, 4 stories and 2,000 square feet was built in 1980 no doubt to the chagrin of its neighbors. Walking along the dock you can view a very beautiful etched glass front door sporting the designs of benevolent dragons. The main floor has a 20 foot ceiling and the upper level is the master bedroom decked out with a marble fireplace. The bathroom has white

marble with brass dolphin fixtures and a mermaid designed in etched glass.

The City of Seattle- Yellow Ferry Harbor

This is one of the oldest wooden hulled ferryboats on the West Coast and is now divided into apartments. This 121 foot "side wheeler" was constructed in Portland, Oregon in 1888 and originally ran on Puget Sound. In her older days of operation she could carry 10 teams and wagons along with 400 passengers. Eventually the wagons gave way to autos when she ran service from Martinez-Benecia in 1913. During World War II the government used her up by Mare Island (North Bay) after which she was "mothballed," until she was brought to Sausalito in 1959.

Strawberry Point (Mill Valley)

If you look across the water from the floating homes community you can see this point. Richardson's Bay continues to the northwest on the left side of this point and to the north along the right side.

The first non-Indian residents on Strawberry Point were

the Lyfords. Dr. Benjamin Franklin Lyford married Hilarita Reed. She was the granddaughter of John Reed (he received an extensive land grant in 1835, including the entire Tiburon Peninsula). Hilarita inherited 1,466 acres of land in Tiburon and 466 acres on Strawberry Point. In 1872 the Lyfords built a house on Strawberry. They were surrounded by their Eagle Dairy that specialized in milk from Jersey cows. It was also here that Doctor Lyford came up with a new embalming method. He died in 1906, and part of the secret formula went with him. His wife died two years later.

In 1945 Strawberry Point was considered as a possible building site of the United Nations. In 1957 money was raised to protect the area of Richardson's Bay between Strawberry

The Lyford House on the Audubon Center grounds in Tiburon with Strawberry Point, Mill Valley in the background.

Pt. and Tiburon to the east against development. The plan had been to fill in much of the tidelands and build 2,000 homes and a couple yacht clubs. Fortunately, this later became the Audubon's Richardson's Bay Wildlife Sanctuary instead.

In 1957, the Lyford house was barged over to its current location across Richardson's Bay from Strawberry Point to the Richardson's Bay Audubon Center & Sanctuary grounds in Tiburon, and has been completely restored.

The Sleeping Princess-Mt. Tamalpais

Looking up from the Sausalito waterfront to the distant mountain to the northwest you are viewing Mt. Tamalpais. Ancient Miwok legend talks of a great rain that threatened to flood the land. The Miwok Chief at the time called to the Great Spirit to help and offered to sacrifice his only daughter, the beautiful Princess Tamal if the Great Spirit helped his people. And so he did, sending beaver and seal, that in turn became two large islands the people could climb up on to escape the rising waters. After the waters receded, beaver and seal became the islands of Yerba Buena and Alcatraz and the people returned to their villages.

The Great Spirit was moved by the love of these people and gave them back the body of Princess Tamal to protect the people

The Indian Maiden in the background with the Richardson's Bay Bridge (Hwy 101) below.

from future floods. The mountain now called Mt. Tamalpais arose, and the silhouette is in the shape of the sleeping princess. There are different ways to look at her outline. One is that the highest peak is her chest and sloping downward to the east is her neck, face and then hair.

The highest peak is approximately 2,600 feet. In 1896 eight mile long railroad tracks were built from Mill Valley up to the summit with 281 hairpin curves. Coming back down was said to be "the longest rollercoaster ride in the world." The tracks were dismantled in the 1930s.

Chapter Eight

Fort Baker & the Marin Headlands

Fort Baker — Located at the southern tip of Sausalito just below and east of the north end of the Golden Gate Bridge.

From downtown Sausalito follow Bridgeway south continuing past old town/Whaler's Cove then a short climb uphill taking a left onto East Road to Fort Baker. Parking is best along Sommerville Road overlooking Horseshoe Cove or alternatively in the Bay Area Discovery Museum parking lot.

Fort Baker today still maintains its age old ambiance with 28 historic buildings (many reflecting colonial revival style architecture) surrounding a central parade ground with a nearby sheltered harbor and old gun batteries. Its early history relates to the San Carlos, the first European ship to sail into the San Francisco Bay in 1775. The Captain was Lt. Juan Manuel de Ayala. After anchoring for several weeks in Ayala Cove at Angel Island and exploring the Bay, the San Carlos pulled up anchor. As the ship sailed out of the Bay stormy conditions pushed it against the rocks at Lime Point (the point just east of the G. G. Bridge's north tower).

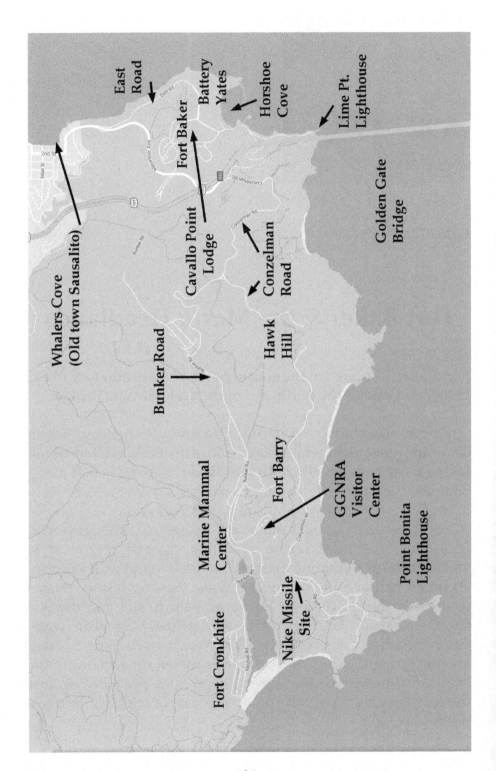

East Road

Battery Yates

Horshoe Cove

Lime Pt. Lighthouse

Fort Baker

Whalers Cove (Old town Sausalito)

Cavallo Point Lodge

Conzelman Road

Golden Gate Bridge

Bunker Road

Hawk Hill

Marine Mammal Center

Fort Barry

GGNRA Visitor Center

Point Bonita Lighthouse

Fort Cronkhite

Nike Missile Site

At that time Lime Point was named Punta de San Carlos by Captain Ayala. The eventual name Lime Point came from the Americans because of the thick coating of bird guano (white lime) covering the rocky point.

The ship's rudder was damaged. The San Carlos sailed shoreward and anchored in what is today called Horseshoe Cove at Fort Baker, remaining there for about ten days while repairs were made.

The next milestone in Fort Baker's history came in 1838 when this area became part of the Mexican land grant awarded William Richardson. Most likely Richardson used this area for cattle grazing. In 1848 the Treaty of Guadalupe Hidalgo was signed ending the Mexican-American War and what is known as Alta (upper) California became part of the United States. This of course was during the Gold Rush. The U.S. Army had the responsibility for protecting San Francisco formerly known as Yerba Buena, and its natural harbor.

Canon emplacements were built at Fort Point, Fort Baker, Fort Mason (S.F.), Alcatraz and Angel Island during the 1850s-60s for defense of the inner harbor. The concept was to provide overlapping fire. These were later replaced by earthen and then concrete batteries.

The U.S. Army-Navy devised a plan to build two forts at the entrance of the Bay, one on the south side and one directly across on the north side where today's Golden Gate Bridge stands. In the end only one fort was constructed (Fort Point on the south side). In part this was due to the fact that the chosen location of the north side fort was at Lime Point. At this time Lime Point was privately owned as part of Richardson's Mexican land grant. It wasn't until 1866 that the governor gained title to what then became known as the Lime Point Military Reservation.

Due to evolving ideas about coastal defenses and newer technologies Fort Point soon became obsolete. This meant that a second fort, similar in defense would never be built across the straits at Lime Point.

Instead the new plan was to construct earthwork batteries. Today around Fort Baker and to the west of the Golden Gate

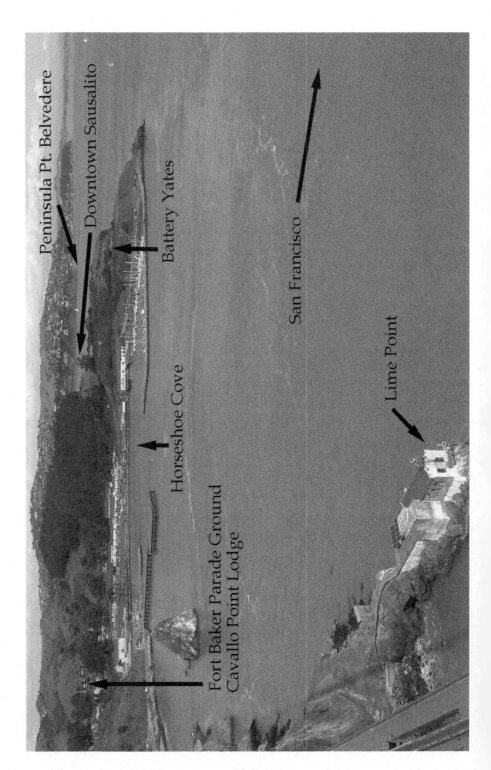

Peninsula Pt. Belvedere

Downtown Sausalito

Battery Yates

San Francisco

Lime Point

Horseshoe Cove

Fort Baker Parade Ground
Cavallo Point Lodge

106

Bridge along the Marin Headlands you can see remnants of these types of coastal defenses. Begun in the 1870s batteries continued to be built with updated technologies up through WWI, WWII and ending with the Cold War era Nike Missile site (SF-88L) at Fort Barry.

One of the earlier batteries which you can visit at Ft. Baker today is Battery Yates. This was/is a concrete battery, one amongst a number built between 1892-1905. It was built with six 3-inch rapid fire guns aimed to protect he inner harbor (the area inside today's Golden Gate Bridge).

In 1897 the Lime Point Military Reservation became known as Fort Baker named in honor of a Civil War colonel (Edward Dickinson Baker). The same year Fort Baker housed the first permanent garrison of soldiers. At that time they lived in tents. In the early 1900s the Army began building permanent housing and warehouse facilities. Many of the buildings you see today around the parade ground date from that time.

Over the years the number of soldiers garrisoned at Fort Baker varied dramatically. During WWI, at one time there were as many as 6,000 soldiers at Fort Baker and Fort Barry (west of the G. G. Bridge in the Marin Headlands). In contrast, between the years 1922-1931 only a small unit of caretakers were stationed

Fort Baker Parade Ground & Cavallo Point Lodge

Battery Yates

there.

Besides housing soldiers assigned to coastal defenses Fort Baker also had other missions. For example, in 1941 the Mine Depot was completed and by 1945 there were approximately 481 submerged mines guarding the entrance to the Bay.

Post WWII Fort Baker continually reinvented itself. At one point there was an Army Laboratory onsite, then the fort became a regional Air Defense Command, a training center, home to a U.S. Corps of Engineers construction unit, housing for soldiers from San Francisco's Presidio fort, and in 1951 the Western Army Anti-Aircraft Command. This was followed by various assignments during the Cold War.

In 1973 Fort Baker was listed in the National Registry of Historic Places. In 2002 the fort was transferred to the National Park Service and the Golden Gate National Recreation Area. In order to generate income and to preserve the historic legacy of Fort Baker, the NPS awarded a contract and the Cavallo Point Lodge took over. As part of the contract 28 historic buildings were rehabilitated and the lodge was opened in 2008.

Having a drink/meal on the veranda outside the lodge's restaurant with stunning views of the Golden Gate Bridge provides for a very romantic setting. The stylish bar inside with its crackling fireplace and original copper ceiling is charming.

Lime Point—Below and just east of the Golden Gate Bridge's north tower.

The brick building resting on Lime Point was constructed in 1883 and included steam powered fog whistles. The steam boilers reportedly consumed 250 pounds of coal each hour during heavy usage when the fog was thick. The whistles themselves were twelve inches in diameter. In 1900 this building was converted into a lighthouse by adding a navigational beacon. In 1961 it was automated.

After construction of the fog house, a keeper's residence was built next to it, and eventually a number of warehouse-type structures (all on Lime Point and the immediate shoreline). In the early 1960s the residence and the warehouses were demolished leaving only the original brick building we still see today.

Besides the San Carlos bashing against Lime Point, in 1901 the iron-hulled steamer the City of Rio de Janeiro hit the rocks here. One hundred and twenty-eight out of 210 passengers died. In 1960 the ship India Bear crashed against the point (while the fog signals were blaring). Damage to the ship was listed as $60,000 and the repair bill for the lighthouse was $7,500.

The Golden Gate or the entrance to San Francisco Bay since the early 1800s has seen 95 wrecks (counting only ships wrecked and sunk). Historically it is considered one of the most treacherous entrances to a Pacific coast harbor second only to the Columbia River.

Besides Fort Baker there were two other army posts in the Marin Headlands. I chose to highlight Fort Baker because it was the first fort in the Marin Headlands, and is also located closer to downtown Sausalito.

The two other forts are Fort Barry and Fort

Cronkhite (both located west of the G.G. Bridge from Fort Baker). The Fort Barry post opened in 1908 and Fort Cronkhite in 1941. Both forts were part of the coast artillery defenses. After touring Fort Baker, a drive or bike ride (for the hearty only), out along the Marin Headlands is an absolute must! Find Conzelman Road, west of the bridge with its sweeping views of the bridge, coastline and open ocean. Along this route you will have opportunities to stop (great for picnics) and see various historic batteries, check out Fort Barry and Fort Cronkhite, take a tour of the historic Pt. Bonita Lighthouse (select hours only), tour the Nike Missile site (limited hours), stop by the GGNRA visitor center, and for a more modern thrill visit the Marine Mammal Center. Below I highlight a few of these sites.

After you explore this area you'll return via Bunker Road up the valley back to the 101 freeway or Sausalito.

Hawk Hill-Marin Headlands on Conzelman Road

Following Conzelman Road to its highest point on the west side of the bridge you'll come to Hawk Hill. From the parking area you can make the short hike up a dirt road to the top. Standing here amongst the remnants of WWII Battery Construction 129

Marin Headlands Looking East To San Francisco

this 923 foot peak offers incredible views of the entrance to the S.F. Bay, the bridge, San Francisco and the East Bay.

Hawk Hill, as the name indicates is a bird watcher's delight. During the late August through December diurnal (daytime) raptors soar overhead on their migratory path. In fact this area is host to the largest diurnal raptor migration amongst the Pacific states, and seasonal counts indicate approximately 29,000 raptors each fall.

Why do they congregate here at the highest peak in the Golden Gate National Recreation Area? The Golden Gate offers one of the narrowest crossings across water along the coast. These birds use warm thermals to give them lift, something that doesn't occur much when flying over the water hence the shortest route is favored. However, the Marin Headlands do provide cold updrafts as the birds climb higher before heading south. The list of raptors here include: Osprey, eagles, harriers, falcons, kites, and hawks. This area is also home to the endangered Mission Blue butterfly.

Point Bonita Lighthouse-Near Field and Mendell Roads
(see resource section)

At land's end this lighthouse (built 1855) was the "last manned lighthouse on the California Coast." With its million dollar views the ½ mile hike down to the lighthouse demonstrates once again why the Marin Headlands (within the GGNRA) is the mesmerizing centerpiece to the outdoor experience in the Bay Area. The hike meanders down a pathway that at one point goes through a tunnel carved through a cliff.

In 1876 Chinese workers who had cut the Sierra tunnels for the transcontinental railroad were brought in to make the 118 foot tunnel that local workman failed at. Once through the tunnel the path leads to a classic looking suspension bridge which you have to cross to reach the lighthouse.

Operated by the U.S. Coast Guard and now automated, the lighthouse was the third one built on the West Coast. The

Marin Headlands Looking West With Pt. Bonita Far Left

population of San Francisco blew wide open during the Gold Rush and there was an evident need to protect against shipwrecks at the entrance to the Golden Gate. The lighthouse was originally built on a higher ridge nearby but the light was often hidden by thick fog. The solution was to move it to its current location in 1877 below the main fog line.

Point Bonita Lighthouse. Photo-Dionigi Pozzi

The lighthouse still uses its original Fresnel lens (invented by Augustus Fresnel in 1822). The Fresnel lens is comprised of glass prisms that direct light horizontally, and can be seen on clear days for 18 miles. Each lighthouse has its own light emitting pattern which enables pilots to know their location.

In addition to the light beam there is a "sound system," originally canon fire but today an electric fog horn. This provides for a back-up when the light is obscured by weather conditions.

Nike Missile Site SF-88L-Near Conzelman and Fields Road
(see resource section)

During the Cold War the U.S. Army constructed around 300 Nike Missile sites throughout the country. This site however, is the only "fully restored" missile site in the U.S.

The Nike missile sites were considered the "last line of defense" against Soviet long range bombers. SF-88L was in operation from 1954-74. Originally equipped with Nike Ajax missiles they were replaced with Nike Hercules missiles. Visiting this site provides for a fascinating but chilling perspective on the Cold War period as you tour below ground missile silos with deactivated full size missiles.

There is another site related to SF-88L and that is the

Integrated Fire Control SF-88C site which is actually to the north on Wolf Ridge. This compound has not been restored but held the computer and radar equipment for tracking targets and guiding the missiles from the launch site.

Chapter Nine

Sausalito Stories

Retrofitting Floating Homes

In the old days many floating homes were built with Styrofoam blocks or fiberglassed pontoons for flotation. These types of material deteriorate faster than the newer type of cement hulls.

Aquamaison, a floating home builder, developed a technique for transferring older floating homes onto new cement barges (hulls). Aquamaison is based in the Sausalito Shipyard and Marina along the Sausalito waterfront.

At low tide they sink the cement barge. The tide then comes in and covers it after which they tow over the floating home and position it over the sunken barge. The floating home is centered over the barge using winches, lines and guides. When the tide goes back out, the home settles onto temporary support walls fixed on the barge walls. Then the water is pumped out of the barge and as the tide comes back in, the whole thing floats. At this point the old flotation is taken out, and the entire structure is re-supported on the cement barge.

Waterproofing and sealing are next. Due to the flexibility of old style flotation, something called hogging or curving happens to many floating homes. As the home is settled onto the new cement barge the home levels out which can crack sheetrock, jam doors and results in stuck windows. This requires additional repairs.

Besides having a reliable hull there's another reason to have a cement barge underneath. The banks will only offer loans to floating homes with a cement hull.

The Mystery Of The Hum

For many years members of the floating homes community were mystified by a strange hum sound heard during the summer months from 9pm to 5am. Some compared it to the droning sound of a B-17 bomber. One resident said the sound came from the water and made his concrete hull vibrate.

A study was done, and they found that the hum had an "unusual frequency spectrum." It was determined that this didn't come from any mechanical/electrical devices. Eventually "the experts" found that the sound came from the California singing fish, aka Plainfin Midshipman.

Midshipmen are nocturnal fish buried in mud or sand during the day. They float above the floor bed at night, and some have venomous dorsal spines. Mating relies on auditory communication from males coming from quick contractions of muscles in the swim bladder. The sound has been described as a hum and can be amplified by the hulls of some boats. The females hear the amorous call and lay their eggs in a rock nest made by the male. All fun and games for the fish, but for floating homes residents it can be hard to sleep.

Floating Homes Wars

During the time that the BCDC first created established legal floating home marinas there were still many people living along the tidal zone plus the anchor-outs. Many of these alternative lifestyle people didn't like the legal marinas because it challenged their independence. Yet they were told that their homes were illegal. This led to the famous houseboat wars back in the '70s. The news channels played footage of cops "jousting boat to boat" with hippies and other salty dogs bent on maintaining their freedom. This went on for over a decade and later moved into the courts.

Older residents of Sausalito will remember that in the mid '80s there was a huge floating barge in the middle of Richardson's Bay towards Belvedere and Cone Rock Buoy. This became a center for the anchor-out lifestyle. A variety of decrepit liveaboard boats were tied up to the dilapidated barge, and some even pitched camp on top of it. There were even two unofficial mayors with a running feud. Authorities had long wished to haul away the old barge and eyesore, but diplomacy made this difficult. The moment came after the mayors fought and one was stabbed. This was the excuse the authorities needed to uphold the law. Within a couple of weeks the anchor-outs and the barge were gone.

The Squatter Of Belvedere Island

Belvedere is approximately one mile by half a mile wide (200 acres). During the years from 1855-1885 Israel Kashow and his family lived here essentially as squatters. The problem was that an Irishman, John Reed claimed that Belvedere was part of his land grant called Rancho Corte Madera del Presidio. This rancho extended from the base of Mt. Tamalpais to the tip of what was then called Point Tiburon (today Peninsula Point, Belvedere). However the land grant did not include islands but just the mainland. After the Bear Flag Revolt in 1846 the U.S. took over the area. One of the first American surveys of the Reed land grant did not include Belvedere. Was it an island or was it part of the mainland?

Back in those days Belvedere was attached to Tiburon by a narrow isthmus which at high tide was at times under water.

Kashow somehow arranged for officials, related to his conflict with the John Reed land grant, to come inspect the area at high tide and therefore Belvedere appeared to be an island and hence not part of the greater rancho.

So for awhile Kashow was safe again. However, another problem arose. The U.S. government had claim over all the islands in the Bay. Legend says that Kashow invited U.S. officials out for an inspection at low tide where the isthmus connecting Belvedere to Tiburon could be seen and therefore Belvedere was not an island.

Eventually, the military took over the area and named it Peninsula Island but Kashow and his family continued to live there. Finally, in 1885 Belvedere was ruled to be part of the Rancho Corte Madera and Kashow was evicted.

The Houseboat Summit 1967 On The Vallejo Ferry

This was a recorded meeting that took place on the Vallejo with counterculture personalities Alan Watts, Timothy Leary, Allen Ginsberg and Gary Snyder. The meeting was recorded for the *San Francisco Oracle Magazine* Issue 7, February 1967. From a modern perspective, listening to these characters pontificate on the counterculture scene, using the language of the '60s, is quite entertaining.

To listen to the online recording go to *youtube.com* and search for *The Houseboat Summit 1967*. Below is a partial transcript.

Watts: *...Look the, we're going to discuss where it's going...the whole problem of whether to drop out or take over.*

Leary: *Or anything in between?*

Watts: *Or anything in between, sure.*

Leary: *Cop out...drop in...*

Snyder: I see it as the problem about whether or not to throw all your energies to the subculture or try to maintain some communication network within the main culture.

Watts: Yes. All right. Now look...I would like to make a preliminary announcement so that it has a certain coherence. This is Alan Watts speaking, and I'm this evening, on my ferry boat, the host to a fascinating party sponsored by the San Francisco Oracle, which is our new underground paper, far-outer than any far-out that has yet been seen. And we have here, members of the staff of the Oracle. We have Allen Ginsberg, poet, and rabbinic saddhu. We have Timothy Leary, about whom nothing needs to be said (laughs) and Gary Snyder, also poet, Zen monk, and old friend of many years.

Ginsberg: This swami wants you to introduce him in Berkeley. He's going to have a Kirtan to sanctify the peace movement. So what I said is, he ought to invite Jerry Rubin and Mario Savio, and his cohorts. And he said: "Great, great, great!" So I said, "Why don't you invite the Hell's Angels, too?" He said: "Great, great, great! When are we gonna get hold of them? So I think that's one next feature...

Leary: I think we should get them to drop out, turn on, and tune in.
Ginsberg: Yeah, but they don't know what that means even.

Leary: I know it. No politician, left or right, young or old, knows what we mean by that.

Ginsberg: Don't be so angry!

Leary: I'm not angry...

Ginsberg: Yes, you are. Now, wait a minute...Everybody in Berkeley, all week long, has been bugging me...and Alpert...about what you mean by drop out, tune in, and turn on. Finally, one young kid said, "Drop out, turn on, and tune in." Meaning: get with an

119

activity--a manifest activity--worldly activity--that's harmonious with whatever vision he has. Everybody in Berkeley is all bugged because they think, one: drop-out thing really doesn't mean anything, that what you're gonna cultivate is a lot of freak-out hippies goofing around and throwing bottles through windows when they flip out on LSD. That's their stereotype vision. Obviously stereotype.

Leary: *Sounds like bullshitting...*

Otis Redding & The Hit Song *Sitting on the Dock of the Bay*

Just after the Monterey Pop Festival in June of 1967 Otis Redding was hanging out on a floating home in Sausalito when he was inspired to write this famous song. While on tour he completed the song and recorded it in a studio in Memphis, Tennessee on December 6 & 7th. On December 10th he and other band members were on a charter plane that crashed and Redding died. In early 1968, The Dock of the Bay was released and went to number one on the R & B charts. Rolling Stone magazine voted it 28 on the top 500 songs of all-time. Redding's song was on the soundtrack for the movie Top Gun.

There are several divergent accounts as to the location of the floating home Redding stayed on in Sausalito. However, based on several resources including Jonathan Gould, the author of *Otis Redding: An Unfinished Life*, it was Main Dock. According to Gould, Redding road manager Speedo Slims, who stayed with Redding on the floating home, confirmed this. The home itself was rented by rock promoter Bill Graham who offered it to Redding for a short stay. Apparently right after Redding left Neil Young was also encamped there.

It is generally agreed that during Redding's stay on the Sausalito waterfront he came up with the idea for the song and several of the lyrics. But the majority of the song was written after he left Sausalito with guitarist Steve Cropper.

Sitting on the Dock of the Bay

Sitting in the morning sun
I'll be sitting when the evening comes
Watching the ships roll in
And I watch 'em roll away again

[Refrain]
Sitting on the dock of the bay
Watching the tide roll away
I'm just sitting on the dock of the bay
Wasting time

I left my home in Georgia
Headed for the 'Frisco bay
'Cause I had nothing to live for
And look like nothing's gonna come my way

So I'm just...
[Refrain]

Look like nothing's gonna change
Everything still remains the same
I can't do what ten people tell me to do
So I guess I'll remain the same

Sittin here resting my bones
And this loneliness won't leave me alone
It's two thousand miles I roamed
Just to make this dock my home

Now, I'm just...
    [Refrain]

William Randolph Hearst And Sausalito

Hearst was born in San Francisco in 1863. Eventually he
went off to Harvard but was kicked out after three years for his

121

constant games. He worked in New York for a while and then returned to San Francisco to run the S.F. Examiner.

As a 23 year old he rented a place in Sausalito and soon his mistress from his Harvard days, Tessie Powers, joined him. Sausalito society (the British colony as it was termed), snubbed Hearst. It seems the local citizens didn't like Hearst's unsanctioned relationship with Tessie. He wasn't invited to join the prestigious San Francisco Yacht Club in Sausalito, which his house overlooked.

Soon he moved into a house nearby at Sea Point and also bought up a number of lots. He had always been intrigued by palaces, castles and the fine art of Europe and dreamed of building a magnificent castle. Construction began in April 1890 near his Sea Point properties. A massive stone and concrete foundation was started, but that was as far as the project went. Today a more modern house sits atop this original Hearst foundation.

Hearst left for Europe but eventually came back. He unsuccessfully attempted to purchase 20 acres of property south of Old Town Sausalito towards Lime Point (north end of the Golden Gate Bridge). Once again he left Sausalito but returned in 1910 and built a Spanish style home and lived there for a time. Hearst never built his castle in Sausalito but eventually did so in San Simeon, California.

Richardson's Bay: What Could Have Been

Sausalito's Panama Canal almost happened. In 1912 there was a proposal to cut a four mile channel from Tennessee Valley Cove (the channel being located on the west side of Richardson's Bay Bridge) over to R.B., thus creating a backdoor shipping canal into the Bay. This idea came up again in 1936 when the Navy was eyeballing R.B. as a potential submarine base. The idea was to avoid the treacherous Potato Patch off the coast as well as the fog drenched entrance at the Golden Gate. The Sausalito City Council liked this idea because for sometime they had wanted to dredge out a deeper channel so ships could travel farther up into R.B. In conjunction with building the canal the Navy would also have to dredge a deeper route along the waterfront. However, the Navy scraped the whole plan.

In December 1935 Joseph Strauss, chief engineer for the Golden Gate Bridge, proposed filling in the northern half of Richardson's Bay to create an amusement park, coliseum and airfield, among other things. Fortunately this idea never materialized. Prior to the 1939 World's Fair another big plan for Richardson's Bay was considered. Officials were looking for a site for the fair and considered dumping bay fill in a large section of the northwestern bay, thinking that once filled and leveled the area could be used for an airport after the fair. In the end, they selected Goat Island shoals next to Yerba Buena Island, filled the area in with massive amounts of bay fill and created Treasure Island.

Admiral Nimitz And Floating Hazards On The Bay

Admiral Chester Nimitz was the Chief Commander of the Pacific Fleet when his seaplane landed on San Francisco Bay in June of 1942. During landing the seaplane struck a "floating hazard" which tore up the undercarriage causing it to flip. The pilot died, but the lucky Admiral received barely a scratch. However, this tragic event led to the Army Corps of Engineers being assigned to clear floating hazards in the Bay. The early vessels for collecting the flotsam and jetsam on the Bay were military tugs. Eventually the Raccoon (docked by the Sausalito Bay Model) was enlisted into service (1959) and still patrols the Bay today.

Sausalito And Highway 101

The construction of the Golden Gate Bridge created a lot of excitement for Sausalito merchants just as had the first train into town. Certain residents proposed running the connecting highway right through the town. Fortunately, the route chosen was the current one known as Waldo Grade. However, in 1946 the California Director of Highways announced three potential plans due to increased traffic on Highway 101. One of the plans was to run a water-level highway along the Sausalito waterfront from the bridge continuing north. Luckily Sausalito residents successfully fought this. By 1951 the highway department decided to enlarge Waldo Grade to handle more traffic. But there was yet another push for a water-level highway around this time by the Northern California Freeway Association. This proposal was defeated and in 1953 work on widening Waldo Grade began.

Chapter Ten

Resource Section

(Parking maps can be found at the end of this resource section.)

Bay Area Discovery Museum

This is an amazing childrens museum with hands-on labs/ exhibits both experiential and educational.

Location: 557 McReynolds Rd., Ft. Baker, Sausalito
Phone: 415-339-3900
Website: bayareadiscoverymuseum.org

Bay Model

The Bay Model is run by the Army Corps of Engineers and is a hydraulic model of the San Francisco Bay and Delta region. The Bay Model serves as an educational center with its numerous information kiosks on the human and natural history of the Bay. Also featured is the *World War II Marinship Exhibit* covering the history of shipbuilding in Sausalito during the war. The model is over 1.5 acres in size. Entrance is free.

Location: Bay Model, Sausalito
Phone: 415-332-3871
Web site: Google-Bay Model, Sausalito

Belvedere-Tiburon Landmark Society (local history)

Location: 1550 Tiburon Blvd. Ste I, Tiburon
Phone: 415-435-5490
Website: landmarkssociety.com

Marin Headlands Visitor Center

Exhibits on the Marin Headlands natural and human history.

Location: Marin Headlands west of the G.G. Bridge near Field and Bunker Roads, Sausalito
Phone: 415-331-1540
Website: Google-Marin Headlands Visitor Center

Marine Mammal Center

Marine Mammal Center has a visitor center as well as a rehabilitation program for injured/sick marine mammals. These are the folks to call if you see injured or sick marine mammals. The center is located in the Marin Headlands. Please note that every year people find seal pups alone onshore thinking they are in trouble. Usually the mother is just out hunting. By removing them from the site they end up being orphaned, and further do not get certain anti-bodies produced by their mother's milk for disease protection.

Location: Marin Headlands west of the G.G. Bridge near Mitchell and Bunker Roads, Sausalito
Phone: 415-289-SEAL (7325)
Web site: tmmc.org

Nike Missile Site SF-88

During the Cold War the U.S. Army constructed around 300 Nike Missile sites throughout the country. This site however, is the only "fully restored" missile site in the U.S.

Location: Marin Headlands west of the G.G. Bridge near Conzelman and Field Roads, Sausalito
Phone: 415-331-1540
Website: Google-Nike Missile Site SF-88
Hours: Limited check website

Point Bonita Lighthouse

At land's end this lighthouse (built 1855) was the "last manned lighthouse on the California Coast." The hike from the parking lot meanders down a pathway that at one point goes through a tunnel carved through a cliff. To reach the lighthouse with its stunning views you'll cross over a classic looking suspension bridge. Sometimes they open on the full moon.

Location: Marin Headlands west of the G.G. Bridge near Field and Mendell Roads, Sausalito
Phone: 415-331-1540
Website: Google-Point Bonita Lighthouse
Hours: Limited check website

Richardson's Bay Audubon Center & Sanctuary

RBACS oversees the 900 acre Richardson's Bay Wildlife Sanctuary. The visitor center and its grounds are located on the northwestern shoreline of R.B. RBACS offers many educational and youth programs. The property is also a great place for a short hike with broad views of R.B. This is also the location of the historic Lyford House.

RBACS is related to the Marin Audubon Society. MAS

was established in 1956 to help stop housing construction on Richardson's Bay tidelands. Their mission statement: To conserve and restore natural ecosystems, focusing on birds, other wildlife, and their habitats, for the benefit of humanity and the earth's biological diversity.

MAS helped found the Audubon Canyon Ranch, protect Bothin Marsh (Mill Valley) and establish the Marin Islands National Wildlife Refuge (MINWR) in San Rafael. MINWR boasts the largest heron rookery in San Francisco Bay. MAS has also purchased and protected thousands of acres of wetland habitat.

Location: 376 Greenwood Beach Rd., Tiburon
Phone: 415-388-2524
Web Site: Google-Richardson Bay Audubon Center

Sausalito Historical Society

Location: Sausalito Civic Center, 420 Litho Street
Phone: 415-289-4117
Website: Sausalitohistoricalsociety.com
Hours: Wednesdays & Saturdays 10-1pm

Sausalito Visitor Center and Historical Exhibit

This is Sausalito's visitor center which is housed in the historic Ice House. A small charming place to learn more about Sausalito history along with fascinating displays and a small bookstore. Open Tuesday through Sunday 11:30-4pm.

Location: 780 Bridgeway, Sausalito
Phone: 415-332-0505
Website: No specific website

Sea Trek Kayak & Stand Up Paddling Center

Based on the water in Sausalito, California's oldest outfitter provides kayak and stand up paddle rentals, guided tours, and instructional classes.

Location: At the Bay Model
Phone: 415-332-8494
Website: Seatrek.com

Wildcare

This visitor center and rehabilitation hospital helps over 3,000 wild animals every year (200 different species). If you find an injured or sick raccoon, rabbit, bird etc. call Wildcare.

Location: 76 Albert Park Lane, San Rafael
Phone: 415-456-7283 (9-5 pm), emergency after hours: 415-300-6359
Website: wildcarebayarea.org

Websites

City of Sausalito
Website: ci.sausalito.ca.us

Sausalito Chamber of Commerce
Website: sausalito.org

Parking

Check out the maps on the next page for help with parking if exploring the tours in this book by car. There are more parking options than listed on the maps but they will give you some ideas, especially when visiting downtown Sausalito which tends to be a lot more hectic. You'll find a combination of free and metered street parking, and pay for municipal lots. The meter maids are looking to write tickets so choose your parking wisely.

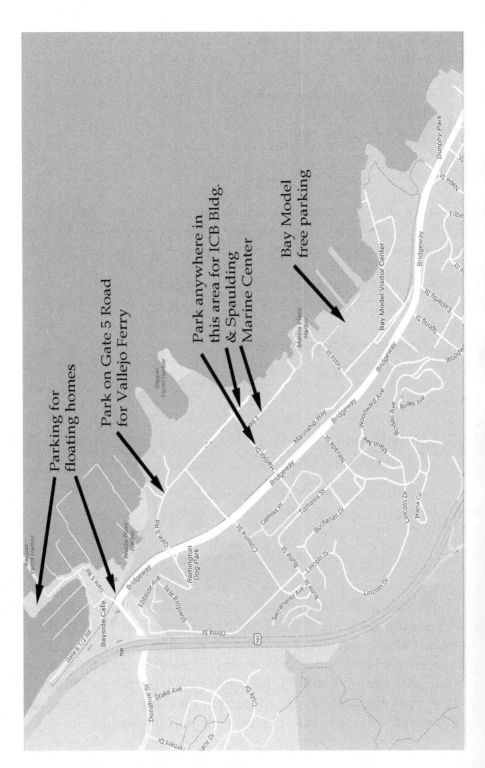

Parking for
floating homes

Park on Gate 5 Road
for Vallejo Ferry

Park anywhere in
this area for ICB Bldg.
& Spaulding
Marine Center

Bay Model
free parking

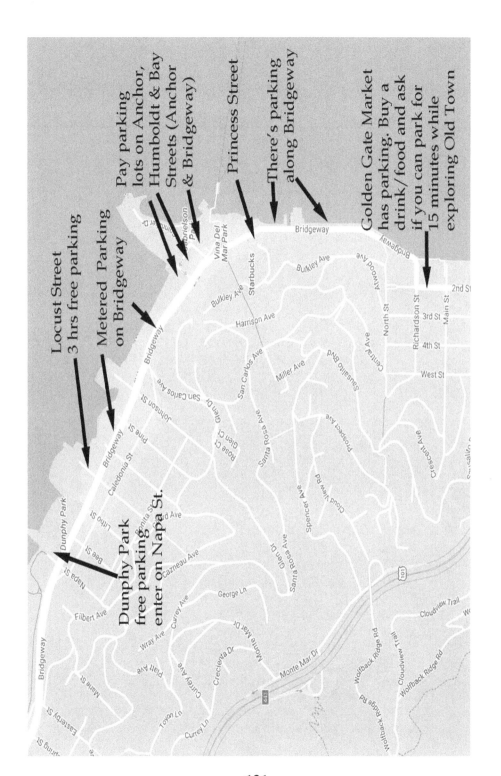

Locust Street
3 hrs free parking

Metered Parking
on Bridgeway

Pay parking
lots on Anchor,
Humboldt & Bay
Streets (Anchor
& Bridgeway)

Princess Street

There's parking
along Bridgeway

Golden Gate Market
has parking. Buy a
drink/food and ask
if you can park for
15 minutes while
exploring Old Town

Dunphy Park
free parking
enter on Napa St.

Made in the USA
Las Vegas, NV
24 April 2022